Jockeys, *Belles* and Bluegrass Kings

Lynn S. Renau

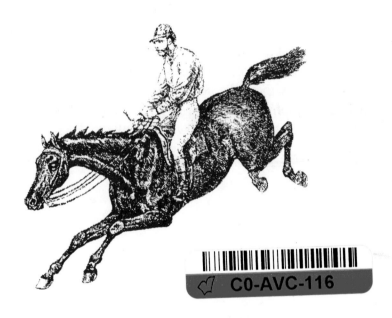

Herr House Press
Louisville, Kentucky

JOCKEYS, BELLES
AND BLUEGRASS KINGS

Acknowledgments

Introduction

Acknowledgments

Myron Estes and Mary Sidney Keiley first got me wondering who made up all those ridiculous stories about Thoroughbred horseracing starting in New York.

Les Shively never stopped telling me to write about racing in south Louisville, where he watched bookmakers come and go at Douglas Park when he was a boy.

Patrick Chapman, *The Courier-Journal*'s Reference Supervisor and Tony Terry, Churchill Down's Director of Publicity, shared their records on Louisville racing, as did the staff of the Louisville Free Public Library, especially Cheryl Jones. I hope *Jockeys, Belles and Bluegrass Kings* rewards their considerable efforts to understand what the sport is all about.

By combining the Filson Club Historical Society's resources with Charles and Mary Todhunter's genealogy of the Churchill family, M. Lewis Clark's life came together. John Harralson, publisher of *The Voice-Tribune*, told his readers a story about "Mrs. Downs" that led me straight to Sallie Ward.

Louisville historian George Yater got me started with racing's roots back in England, then Keeneland Library's Doris Waren and Kathy Schenck kept me on the right track close to home. Lexington historian Burton Milward researched the Bluegrass tales.

Forty years ago at Collegiate School, Virginia Wittmeier taught history and Alberta Anderson cooked lunch. I still can't decide which subject I like best. Alice Colombo, *The Courier-Journal*'s Food Stylist, made sure all the recipes work.

Agnes Crume patiently edited this book.

Julian Logan "Buck" Wheat, Bill Chenault, Dixon "Tat" Tatgenhorst, Margo Grace and Julius Berry, God bless 'em, have been my cheering squad for the last four years.

Lastly, there is Churchill Downs Inc. Vice President, Corporate Communications Karl F. Schmitt, Jr. who, after I outlined this project for him in 1991, told me "Lynn, you can do all the research, but no woman is ever gonna write a history of this race track!" then hedged his bet by letting me have press passes every year!

Introduction

Late in 1987, Leslie Combs gave the Kentucky Derby Museum his collection of racing trophies. The Brown Foundation funded The Trophy Room — to display Combs' trophies, along with those won by Jack Price's Carry Back, and J. Graham Brown's Brown Hotel Stables. Early in 1988, the museum's director called me. Would I put the Trophy Room project together? The work required no knowledge of racing, he hastened to add. I agreed to meet him for lunch, then had to ask for directions to Churchill Downs! That project stretched to five years — time enough to meet hotwalkers, exercise riders, jockeys, trainers and horse owners. To a person, they were incredible, cockeyed optimists, working long hours, taking risks, loving what they did.

At the museum, I answered the phone a lot. Especially around Derby, callers didn't waste time on introductions. "I need help!" they'd say. "All I want is the answer to one simple question. I've called everywhere. Nobody knows anything." Racing, I realized, is not a user-friendly game. In a sport so competitive it measures success by a nose, wins with a camera, and workouts to 1/5 of a second, there is no visitors' guide to the show, no history of what makes every horse race, whether it's the Derby or a contest for cheap claimers, an act of courage and faith — and fist-waving, foot-stomping fun.

I remember Cecil Bernis, a shy man, part of Churchill Downs' grounds crew, who smiled and waved to me for over a year before he ever spoke. "Museum lady," he finally said, "I hear you write things. Write about us, tell people out there who we are and what racing means to us." Then he walked away, leaving a yellowed newspaper clipping in my hand. Cecil had gone into a burning barn to rescue horses. He saved several horses before the flames won.

This book is for Cecil; jockey Sam Alexander; clocker Kenny Ransom; Bobby Peck, the Clerk of Scales; Kentucky Derby Museum staff, and an exercise rider who always wore a strand of pearls. The famous and the anonymous, they're all part of a world and a sport to which they contribute something wonderfully courageous and foolhardy — the guts to show up and keep working, no matter what the odds.

Jockeys, *Belles* and **Bluegrass Kings**

Chapter One

Hobby to Thoroughbred

Thirty years before Columbus discovered America, Englishmen were both racing and exporting fast, pony-sized Irish horses called "hobbys." When England's King Richard III, alone on the battlefield, cried, "A horse! A horse! My kingdom for a horse!", no Hobby sped to his rescue. Richard's death in 1485 ended the Wars of the Roses — a century of civil conflict — and brought Henry Tudor to the throne.

As early as 1140, the first of a long line of kings named Henry tried to improve Hobby horses by importing Arab stallions to give them "bottom" — speed and staying power. During the Crusades, from 1096 to 1270, Turkish cavalry horses ran circles around the big warhorses English soldiers took with them to the Middle East. Crusaders bought, or captured, Turkish horses to bring home.   T h e n the Wars of the Roses all but destroyed England's horse population. Rebuilding the cavalry was Henry's top priority. To protect what few animals remained, he forbade their exportation. His son, much-married Henry VIII, imported horses from Italy, Spain and North Africa. He kept a racing stable, under the direction of a nobleman called the Master of the Horse. Henry's Hobbys, as well as his imported Arab stallions, raced against horses owned by the nobility, in matches arranged for the entertainment of the court. Eventually the word "Hobby" came to mean a costly pastime indulged in by the idle rich. Henry's stables were supported by tax revenues; racing was justified because winners were bred to winners to "improve the breed." Geldings weren't allowed to compete. Henry's Master of the Horse was not a professional horseman, consequently, by the time Henry died, his horses had been so indiscriminately crossbred, the royal stable was no more than a jumbled lot of animals with very muddled genes. These horses were called "cocktails," from which we get our word for a mixed drink.

Elizabeth I, Henry's daughter, set about remedying the situation. First she got rid of horses not suited for racing or the cavalry, then she stabled the best of Henry's Hobby and Arab stock in new barns at Tutbury near Staffordshire. There, matings were carefully planned and pedigrees systematically recorded. Elizabeth ruled England for fifty years. Unlike her father, she never married and seldom let friendships interfere with the business of government, international trade or domestic commerce.

On the advice of her Master of the Horse, Gervase Markham, Elizabeth added Arabs, "little Horses, verie swift," sometimes referred to as Barbarians, to her stables. Markham urged his fellow Englishmen to breed Arab stallions to Hobby and Galloway (Scottish) mares because their offspring showed "wonderful speede in both short and long courses." If "plaine bredde" mares showed promise, these mares, with names like Miss Darcy's Pet Mare or Daughter of Snake, were added to the pedigree records owners kept for themselves.

At Elizabeth's death, James VI of Scotland, son of Mary Queen of Scots, whom Elizabeth had ordered beheaded, inherited the English throne, uniting the countries. James fancied himself a great sportsman. He attended the races at Newmarket regularly and thought nothing of being seen there two weeks after his wife died of dropsy. When his son, Charles, became king in 1625, he not only supported Newmarket, he expanded the palace and royal racing stables James had built nearby. Charles eventually ran afoul of Parliament for his excessive spending and arrogant ways. By 1642, England was at war again. After Puritan leader Oliver Cromwell's army defeated Charles' Cavaliers in 1647, Charles fled to Scotland, but Scottish leaders returned him to England, where he was convicted of treason and beheaded two years later.

When Cromwell captured the royal stables at Tutbury, he inventoried all the horses there. His advisors determined that most of the so-called Royal Mares, descended from Hobbys, Galloways and Arabs, should be sold. Fewer than 100 were kept — not for racing, but in hopes of producing strong, lighter-weight animals for the cavalry. Gunpowder had long since made slow, armored war horses obsolete.

Cromwell's Councils of State passed law after law prohibiting racing, but matches were held nonetheless. When the government retaliated by confiscating horses, pedigree records were again lost. Royalists and Cavaliers were forced to leave England, or banished to their country estates, where they kept records of the horses they bred for staghunting and racing, waiting for Englishmen to tire of repressive religious rule. Long-exiled Charles II became king two years after Cromwell died.

Charles married a Portuguese princess whose dowry included the North African port city of Tangier, giving him access to all the Barbary Coast horses he wanted. North Africans wouldn't export mares, but they were eager to sell their surplus stallions, which their religion did not permit them to geld. Charles, accompanied by his popular mistress, Nell Gwynn, became a prominent figure at the Newmarket races, where he jockeyed his own horses, set down rules and arbitrated disputes. Charles' participation made racing England's "Sport of Kings." Before Charles' death 21 years later, a horse "thorough bred" for racing had emerged from England's stud farms. By 1700, aristocratic breeders and businessmen were all in competition to produce pedigreed champions.

Charles' successors, William III, and Queen Anne, were avid racing fans. During their reigns, tracks sprang up all across England. Even an equine flu epidemic didn't dampen English racing fever for long. Queen Anne's contribution to the sport was the Ascot course, near Windsor Castle, which opened in 1711. The Queen died the day after her horse, Star, won a race there in 1714.

Since none of her 17 children survived her, a distant German cousin inherited the throne, reigning as George I. George, a dullard who never learned English, disliked both his subjects and their pastime, but it made no difference. By then, thoroughbred horses were established in fact and pedigree.

It's no coincidence that all Thoroughbreds trace their pedigrees to Barbary stallions brought to England after 1662, when king and commoner alike loved racing. These horses, with their odd-sounding names — Curwen Bay Barb, St. Victor's Turk, Belgrade Turk and Croft's Egyptian — came from North Africa via France and southeastern Europe. The three best — the Byerley Turk, the Darley Arabian and the Godolphin Arabian — became immortals of the turf.

In 1688, Captain Byerley captured a Turkish officer's horse at the Battle of Buda in Hungary. Byerley rode the Arab stallion throughout the war, then sent him to stud. From the Byerley Turk came Herod, and through him, Diomed, the first Epsom Derby winner.

The Darley Arabian was some 20 years younger than the Byerley Turk. Thomas Darley, a government official at Aleppo, a North African port city, sent the horse to his brother, a Yorkshire horse breeder. Darley's Arabian sired Bartlett's Childers, which sired

Squirt — so-named because of his size — sire of Marske, sire of Eclipse. Another Bartlett's Childers' son was Bulle Rock, the first thoroughbred shipped to colonial Virginia.

The Godolphin Arabian is by far the best-known, although the least important in terms of lasting impact on the breed. Children who've read Marguerite Henry's *King of the Wind* can recite Godolphin's tale of woe by heart. He was foaled in Yemen around 1724, exported via Syria to Tunis, then sent to Louis XV of France, whose royal stable master rejected him. More than a century after the Godolphin died, Victorian writers reduced readers to tears with a story, true or not, that told of Godolphin's descent to the streets of Paris where an English Quaker found him, starving, barely able to stand, hitched to a water cart.

His rescuer, Edward Coke of Derbyshire, was said to have recognized nobility in the poor beast's sunken eyes. Coke bought him, along with his faithful Blackamoor groom, and sent the pair to England. At first, Godolphin was used as a teaser, a stallion used to excite mares prior to mating. Then he fell in love with the beautiful Roxana and fought for her, so the story goes, vanquishing the stallion to which she was to be bred. From their second mating in 1734, came Cade, sire of Machem. The Godolphin, named for the Earl of Godolphin who purchased him from Coke, was a creature of intense emotion. His constant companion was a cat, Grimalkin. After Grimalkin's death, Godolphin hated cats and tried to kill any that got near him. The last great names in Godolphin's line were Man o' War and Man o' War's son, 1937 Triple Crown winner, War Admiral.

During the 1700s, thoroughbred racing lost, with one notable exception, any direct ties to the Crown, but its popularity as a sport grew by leaps and bounds. Only champions were needed to make it supreme. Three horses, born between 1748 and 1764, stamped thoroughbreds with the mark of greatness. They were Matchem, from the Godolphin; Herod, the Byerley Turk's offspring; and Eclipse, from the Darley Arabian line. Ironically, both Herod and Eclipse were bred by the Duke of Cumberland, the only member of the royal family active in 18th Century English racing.

William Augustus, Duke of Cumberland, third son of George II, became a national hero when he defeated flamboyant Scottish rebel leader, Bonnie Prince Charlie, at the Battle of Culloden in 1746. Then his willingness to let his soldiers rape and pillage Scottish villages earned him the nickname "butcher." After he further disgraced himself in Europe, Cumberland was forced to resign. The obese, unpopular Duke withdrew to Windsor Park and started breeding horses, which he raced at the nearby Ascot course. Because of Cumberland's royal connections, he became the unofficial head of the Jockey Club. Both Herod and Eclipse (born on Allfools Day, 1764, when a solar eclipse blackened the earth at noon) were foaled at Cumberland's Windsor Park Stud. Herod was only average as a racehorse, but he was extremely successful as a sire.

After Cumberland's death in 1765, a well-to-do farmer bought Eclipse. The hard-to-handle colt wasn't raced until he was five. But when Eclipse finally made it to the track, it was "Eclipse first, the rest nowhere," racing slang meaning a horse won by at least 240 yards — a distance so great judges couldn't see the second-place horse when the winner crossed the finish line. With no horse owners willing to challenge Eclipse, his racing career lasted only two years. After 1771, he sired crop after crop of champions. When he died, he was mourned as a national hero.

The 44-year-old Cumberland's death caused no such grief, but his name can still be found on Kentucky maps. Today, as when Cumberland was a hero and Dr. Thomas Walker first explored western Virginia, travelers pass through a scenic natural gap in the Appalachians, where Virginia, Tennessee and Kentucky meet. This gateway west, through which so many settlers made their way into the Bluegrass, Walker named for the Duke, before time tarnished Cumberland's reputation and he withdrew to Windsor Park to breed horses whose descendents would make the region famous.

One last step was required to legitimized thoroughbreds. Pedigree records had to be gathered together and published. In 1773, the Jockey Club authorized its newly-appointed Keeper of the Match Book, James Weatherby — who got the job by stealing his competitor's record books — to publish an annual Calendar of racing events. Eighteen years later, Weatherby reluctantly put together the *Introduction to a General Stud Book*, a listing of thoroughbred pedigrees that made them a breed of their own. Weatherby revised this Thoroughbred "Who's Who" in 1793 and it has been kept up-to-date by the Weatherby family ever since.

Americans had no reason to copy Weatherby. At best, American Thoroughbreds developed as cousins of their English ancestors, rooted in the Old World, but bred in the New.

Sir Charles Bunbury

Chapter Two

Gentlemen's Sport

When English aristocrats established Jamestown in 1607, they brought no horses with them. They ate the horses sent to the colony three years later to keep from starving to death. As they prepared to abandon their ill-conceived venture in the New World, more men and horses arrived. By 1649, the year Charles I was beheaded, there were 200 horses in Virginia. Twenty years later, Virginians were selling horses to other New World settlements. Colonists along the costs made contact with Cherokees, Creeks, Choctaws and Seminoles whose Chickasaw ponies descended from Spanish horses, and bred them to their Hobbys and Arabs. This downsized horses so much, owners were ordered to keep their pint-sized stallions away from English mares.

Quarter racing two horses running full speed for a quarter-mile — became a popular Southern pastime. Bumping, crossing paths and savagely whipping opponents was all part of the game. Records of this frontier sport exist because bettors sometimes went to court to settle debts. Men in the Roanoke Valley, the eastern counties on either side of the Virginia-North Carolina border, bred such outstanding quarter horses that the area was called "the Old Race Horse Region." John Randolph of Roanoke, descended from one of the first families of Virginia, was both a thoroughbred and quarter horse man. Luck favored him when he imported Janus — a stallion with Godolphin blood — and bred him to native mares. Janus' offspring were the best short-distance horses in the state, but they had no staying power in distance races.

Puritanical New Englanders and Pennsylvania Quakers had horses, but they wanted no part of Southern racing. Some Northern cities outlawed racing altogether; men with time on their hands were encouraged to bowl, ice skate or play football — sports Virginia gentlemen viewed with contempt.

The first race for which a trophy still exists, but by no means the first American racing, took place in 1665 at a Long Island track built by New York's colonial Governor, Sir Richard Nicholls. Nicholls assured citizens who frowned on racing that it was "not so much for the divertisement of youth as for encouraging the bettering of the breed of horses." At Nicholl's track, stout Dutch horses carried their 140-pound riders over a two-mile course, and there was lots of betting — but only to encourage breed development!

New Yorkers, already at political and religious odds with the aristocratic Nicholls, wanted no part of flat racing. Throughout the 1700s, race meets were held from time to time in New York, but thoroughbreds were too thin-skinned for the cold northern climate. After the Revolution, postwar racing was little more than an excuse to gamble. In 1802, New York outlawed racing and closed every track in the state. There was no more racing there until the Union Course opened near Brooklyn in 1821.

Northerners wanted strong, even-tempered work horses, the opposite of Thoroughbreds. Right after the American Revolution, Justin Morgan, a school teacher, was given a horse ideally suited to New England ways. Some claim Figure, the first Morgan, was sired by True Briton, a Maryland-bred stallion with considerable Thoroughbred blood, but more than likely he came from Fresian stock brought over by German soldiers during the war. Farmers and shopowners hitched Morgans and trotters to buggies and measured their horses' worth by the time and distance they worked in harness. Racing against the clock was dull compared to quarter horse racing, since it provided no opportunity for betting or cheating, but it kept Yankee farmers entertained and in good graces with their church.

Mambrino, an imported stallion descended from Darley's Arabian, and Mambrino's son, Messenger, were purposely bred to Narragansett Pacers to create the ideal horse — the businesslike, tractable Standardbred. By the time the Union Course opened, trotting races — the horses were ridden by their owners — had become too popular to ignore. Gradually, owners hitched their trotters to light-weight, big-wheeled sulkies, and harness racing came into its own.

Thus Virginia and North Carolina gave birth to quarter horse racing and the Standardbred developed in the North, but neither was the Sport of Kings. Thoroughbred racing became part of America's heritage when Cromwell's government forced Royalists and Cavaliers to leave England, taking their wealth, customs and traditions with them. Once these families established themselves on vast tracts of land in Virginia, Maryland and South Carolina, they started importing thoroughbreds. They also enslaved Africans, a race whose knowledge of hot-blooded horses predated that of their masters by centuries.

By 1700, Virginia had the largest population of any colony. Half a century later, the tobacco crops that supported Virginia plantations had worn out the soil, making it was useless for farming. Looking for land, families moved west, while less adventurous Virginians migrated to towns and learned trades.

Enterprising farmers converted useless tobacco fields into dirt racetracks, an idea unheard of in England, where the cultivation of turf courses was already an advanced art. Civic-minded businessmen laid out a mile-long circular track near Williamsburg, then Virginia's capital, and soon horse racing became an annual, seasonal activity in their lives. Visitors with money in their pockets outnumbered residents two-to-one during the racing season. Virginia's Royal Governor encouraged plantation owners to import topnotch horses and race them. It was good for business back home. As early as 1727, prizes for spectators at the Hanover, Va., track included "a hat to be cudgelled for; a violin to be played for; a pair of silver buckles to be wrestled for; a pair of shoes to be danced for; a pair of silk stockings for the handsomest young county maid."

Colonial horses were still small, about 14.2 hands or 58 inches to the withers — the size of a large pony today. In 1730, Virginia tobacco planter Samuel Gist imported Bulle Rock, 21-year-old son of the Darley Arabian, the first true thoroughbred brought to America. Dabster, Crab, and Monkey followed in the 1740s. Twenty-two-year-old Monkey not only survived the trip but sired 300 colts before he died. Virginia's mild climate and green pastures seemed to re-invigorate these elderly animals. Breeders added three more outstanding stallions to Virginia stud rosters in the 1750s when they imported Jolly Roger, Morton's Traveller and Janus. But Fearnought, imported by John Baylor of Caroline County, was far and away the most important thoroughbred that came to America before the Revolution. Baylor loved racing so much he named his Virginia plantation "Newmarket." He already owned Crab, but Crab was too small, so Baylor's British agent shipped Fearnought to Newmarket in 1764. The powerful young stallion stood nearly 16 hands tall and he was very fertile.

Eight years later, stud services of 32 Fearnought sons were being advertised in newspapers around the region. In 1765, an English officer wrote home, bragging: "There are established races annually at almost every town and considerable place in Virginia. Very capital horses are started here."

George Washington managed a track in Alexandria, Va., and trained horses at Mount Vernon both before, and after, the Revolution. Racing horses was a way of life in the South, but keeping track of pedigrees was another matter entirely. By 1793, James Weatherby had published his *General Stud Book* — the bible of British pedigree — but there was nothing like it in America. Jockey club members in Maryland, Virginia and the Carolinas were interested in profitable racing, not record keeping. It didn't matter whether their Arabian-Hobby-Choctaw-Chickasaw "thoroughbreds" were acceptable in English racing circles or not. Nobody planned to return to the Mother Country and find out. Pedigree information, what there was of it, traveled by word-of-mouth, so all horse traders had to do was change horses' names as they traveled from town to town. In the South, what you saw was what you got.

Southern planters continued importing fashionably-bred English stallions, as well as other luxuries, until the end of the 1760s, when something had to give. By then, they owed more money to London merchants than they could ever repay. Between 1770 and the July 4, 1776 signing of the Declaration of Independence, they went right on biting the hand that fed them, piling up debts. If spending had to be scaled back, the stable was the place to do it, especially with stallions the caliber of Fearnought's sons in their barns.

As the nation's mood grew more belligerent, colonial congresses, where Northern anti-racing sentiments were well represented, advised colonies to cut out all forms of extravagance, especially horse racing. Southern aristocrats paid no attention to these warnings. For them, racing way of life — and excellent preparation for war. Everything depended on a successful revolution. It meant, above all, relief from their foreign debts.

After Massachusetts militia fired the opening shot of the Revolution at the Battle of Lexington in the spring of 1775, colonial councils discouraged any activity that took men and horses away from the war effort. Once fighting began in deadly earnest, and the number of British victories grew, thoroughbreds became part of the military. From what survived, or what was imported when the war ended, thoroughbred breeding had to begin all over again.

Ironically, while Americans were fighting for independence, Englishmen developed "the Darby," for which Kentucky is best known today. In September 1776, British race-goers saw the first St. Leger, a race planned the year before by a group of young gentlemen dining near the Doncaster track. Named for an army officer, the St. Leger was an end-of-season, winner-take-all, nearly two-mile sweepstakes, limited to three-year-old colts and fillies — fast-paced entertainment that made betting easy. There was no waiting through three heats to find out which horse won.

Senior Jockey Club members took notice. In 1778, Edward Stanley, twelfth Earl of Derby, suggested a mile-and-a-half contest for fillies. Named the Oaks, after his country retreat near Epsom, it was run in June 1779. Derby's filly, Bridget, won the race. More than likely, Bridget was a promising two-year-old when Derby proposed the event. The success of the Oaks led to plans for a mile-long race — lengthened to a mile-and-a-half in 1784 — at Epsom, open to colts and fillies, to be run in the spring of 1780.

As legend has it, after Lord Derby and a fellow Jockey Club member, Sir Charles Bunbury, set the terms of the race, they agreed the event should be named for one of them, the decision to be made on the toss of a coin. Happily, the coin fell to Derby, or there might be no Kentucky Derbys and a Kentucky Bunbury instead! Bunbury's colt, Diomed, won that first Epsom Derby, but little else in his brief racing career. Diomed was sent to stud, where he spent 20 years in well-deserved obscurity.

The St. Leger, the Oaks and the Epsom Derby were not events beleaguered colonists took note of. For them, 1780 was the lowest point of the war. Charleston fell to British troops weeks before the first English Derby was run. Another defeat at Camden, S.C., two months later, virtually wiped out an entire American army. The biggest victory of 1779 had been Virginia-born Gen. George Rogers Clark's daring military adventures in the British-held Northwest Territory.

Only those possessed of a crystal ball would have known that, 96 years after Clark's capture of the British forts at Kaskaskia, Cahokia and Vincennes, a Thoroughbred with Diomed blood would win the first Kentucky Derby in Louisville — a race whose creation owed so much to the work of the General's great-nephew, Meriwether Lewis Clark, Jr., and Clark's Churchill kin.

The Revolutionary War opened Kentucky, Virginia's westernmost county, to immigrants and colonists alike. By 1785, pioneer wagons were pouring through the Cumberland Gap into south and central Kentucky as flatboats brought settlers down the Ohio River to settle along the Kentucky shoreline. No land proved more hospitable to Thoroughbreds than the Bluegrass region of the state and no cities more amenable to racing than Lexington and Louisville.

In Kentucky, racing flourished as never before.

Diomed

Keeneland Race Course, Lexington Kentucky, 1936

CLUB HOUSE AND GRAND STAND, LATONIA, KENTUCKY.

Latonia Race Track, Latonia Kentucky, 1909

Chapter Three

Shank's Mare, Iron Horses and Jets

Long before Patrick Henry declared, "Give me liberty or give me death," the combination of population growth, coastal land misuse and European immigration sparked the move west. Something in the character of men such as Daniel Boone and George Rogers Clark, along with tens of thousands of unsung pioneers, brought them to the frontier. Most settlers came to Kentucky on "Shank's mare" — by foot.

When hunters camping along a branch of the Elkhorn Creek got news, in June 1775, of the Battle of Lexington the preceding April, they named their campsite Lexington. The Revolution determined who controlled the vast wilderness then under British rule. With the signing of the peace treaty in 1783, what had begun as a migratory trickle into Kentucky, developed into a steady flow. A decade later, 15 roads from all around the state led to Lexington, Ky., "the Athens of the West."

Kentucky attracted not only settlers from the southeastern coastal regions, but newly-arrived immigrants from the north of England, Ireland and Scotland. These often-threadbare men and women, with their clan allegiances and stubborn sense of independence, quickly found themselves at odds with better educated, more aristocratic pioneers who believed that those of lesser rank should always defer to gentlemen and not vote, bet, or race horses. This view of democracy was short-lived in the wilderness where there were no sheriffs to prevent a man from racing his own horses, or betting. As long as wagers were paid, who cared about a man's ancestry?

Just beyond the main thoroughfare in many Kentucky settlements — Louisville being a notable exception because it had a race track early on — there was a Race Street, a straight stretch named for what went on there. Delegate Daniel Boone introduced the first bill "to improve the breed of horses in the Kentucky territory" at the 1775 Transylvania Convention held at Harrodsburg. Quarter path racing in Harrodsburg took place on what was later named Factory Street, a straight stretch near the fort.

As early as 1787, the Commons near Lexington's Race Street became a gathering place for horsemen after safety-minded citizens objected to horses racing on Main Street. Two years later, the Lexington newspaper announced plans for a formal race meet. Kentucky's first jockey club was organized there in 1797, then reorganized as the Lexington Jockey Club in 1809 with statesman Henry Clay as a founding member.

Throughout Kentucky, men such as Revolutionary War veteran William Whitley built handsome Georgian-style houses on land purchased from the government. Whitley was known for his hatred of all things British. When he laid out the dirt track that circled a hill near his monogrammed brick home in Crab Orchard, he decreed that, since the British raced their horses clockwise, horses would run counter-clockwise around his track, a custom that caught on in the South long before the 65-year-old Whitley died fighting in the War of 1812.

Fortunately for the Thoroughbred, the population shift into the Bluegrass occurred as Virginia horsemen struggled under the double burden of religious censure and bad business practices. Those who disapproved of gambling, principally Baptists and Presbyterians, wanted racing outlawed, but that was only part of the problem. Right after the treaty ending the Revolution was signed, British horse dealers started shipping their worst horses to Virginia to replace animals lost in the war. Thoroughbreds brought top dollar because of their pedigrees. One or two were truly superior animals, such as Medley, purchased from renowned British horse merchant Richard Tattersall in 1784. Medley's offspring were the best racehorses of their day. But few sellers were as ethical as Tattersall so Virginia markets were soon flooded with worthless stock.

The rigors of the trip to Kentucky weeded out all but the fittest animals, but the damage done to Virginia's horse industry was irreparable. By the time years of maritime skirmishing with Britain grew into the War of 1812, most breeders had recognized the error of their ways. Few English horses were imported after 1806.

Ironically, and certainly not by design, from this era of deceit came the most extraordinary Thoroughbred sire ever to set foot in Virginia — Sir Charles Bunbury's 1780 Epsom Derby winner, Diomed. After his Derby victory, Diomed's racing career had been lackluster at best. Bunbury sent Diomed to stud in England, where he sired mediocre horses remembered mainly for their bad dispositions. By 1798, the 21-year-old horse was considered useless, suitable only for American trade. Diomed arrived in Virginia in 1800.

Maybe it was the food, or the mild climate, or the Medley mares to which he was bred — something revived Diomed. He became Virginia's undisputed champion sire as soon as his first crop of foals hit the race track. The list of race winners and influential stallions he sired grew every year. When Diomed died at the ripe old age of 31, his loss was regarded as a great natural disaster. There was almost as much grief over Diomed's demise as there had been at the death of George Washington — and with good reason. As a foundation sire, Diomed was worth his weight in gold. His name appears in the pedigree of Aristides, the 1875 Kentucky Derby winner.

The first imported stallion advertised in the Bluegrass was Blaze. Horse and owner went back to Virginia when nobody would pay the man $12 in cash, or value in whiskey, for Blaze's services. A wealthy Scott County farmer, Col. Robert Sanders, purchased Melzar from Virginia horse breeder, Col. John Hoskins, in 1800. Sanders paid $4,000 — 10 times the going rate for a stallion — for this son of Medley. By then, Sanders' Great Crossings Baptist Church had excommunicated him for building a race path near his tavern! Melzar's stud fee was "$30 the leap" — a considerable sum in those days. Sanders' investment died in 1801, but 30 years later Melzar was still regarded as the most important Thoroughbred in the state, although he sired only one crop of foals.

The War of 1812 took a heavy toll on horses. Afterwards, racing was slow to recover in the South and reformers shut it down entirely in the East and North. But Lexington, Ky., always had a track where owners competed their best homebreds. Horsemen quickly realized there was no equal to the Bluegrass when it came to nurturing pedigreed stock. The rolling landscape, untouched by Ice Age glaciers, had been millions of years in the making. Situated between two vast coal fields, continually squeezed and lifted upward until it became a plateau atop a pure limestone base, the Bluegrass was blessed with a mild climate and adequate rainfall. The soil was among the richest in the country and there were clear, spring-fed streams throughout the region.

Bluegrass, technically *Poa pratensis*, is a deep-rooting, thin-bladed hardy perennial, native to the steppes of the Black Sea. Some credit Quaker leader William Penn with its importation, but the seed probably came to America in the pockets of Mennonites ousted from Russia, for whom Pennsylvania was a safe haven before they headed west. Whatever its origin, bluegrass, fed by the high levels of phosphoric acid, potash, lime and magnesium, flourished in the Maury loam silt, providing abundant food and well-cushioned turf for livestock.

Settlers quickly cleared land, maximizing the pasture available for grazing not just horses, but hogs, sheep and cattle — animals with English pedigrees every bit as impressive as Thoroughbreds'. There were few Kentucky farms more productive than those situated within and around the original boundaries of Fayette County — today Fayette, Woodford, Jessamine and Bourbon Counties.

In 1826, 60 prominent Bluegrass businessmen organized the Kentucky Association for the Improvement of Breeds of Stock. They collected the pedigree records of their imported sheep and cattle, but their concerted efforts to untangle the web of Thoroughbred breeding came to naught. There was no centralized breed registry the equivalent of Weatherby's *General Stud Book* until Lexington native Col. Sanders D. Bruce compiled the *American Stud Book* in 1868.

The first Kentucky Association races took place at the mile-long, circular, Old Williams Track in Lee's Wood — site of Lexington Cemetery today — before a course was laid out at Fifth and Race Streets, within easy reach of downtown Lexington. That course originally meandered for four hilly miles, much like its English counterparts. It was remodeled in 1832, becoming America's second mile-long, fenced, dirt track.

A Maryland-born Transylvania medical school graduate, Dr. Elisha Warfield, served as the Kentucky Association's chief trustee. The fabulous horse Lexington, a Diomed descendent, and sire of legendary runners such as Kentucky, Asteroid, General Duke and Tom Bowling, was foaled on Warfield's farm, next door to the track.

By 1850, landlocked Lexington lacked only one thing: a railroad system with direct access to Ohio River trade. The lack of cheap transportation greatly handicapped farmers whose incomes were linked to their ability to ship horses, tobacco, whiskey and perishable produce around the country. As trade became all-important, Lexington was forced to depend on the Louisville & Nashville Railroad, Louisville's "iron horse," for its needs.

In contrast, Louisville, the swampy, riverfront settlement named for France's King Louis XVI, had developed from Portland, where the treacherous Falls of the Ohio frequently forced hapless travelers ashore. From the beginning, Louisville was a brawling river town, home to successive waves of German and Irish immigrants making their way up river from New Orleans. They became hardworking citizens, but they had no desire, or money, to buy Thoroughbreds.

Townspeople with English roots, organized as the Louisville Jockey Club, arranged Thoroughbred matches down by the river at the Hope Distillery turf course near Portland, after racing on Market Street became hazardous. On the east side of the county, pioneer Peter Funk built a racetrack, site of wall-to-wall shopping centers at Taylorsville Road and Hurstborne Lane today. Both tracks were well-patronized. A traveler coming in from Shelby County wrote to his brother in 1829, complaining about the "dirty mechanics who crowded in the stagecoach at Middletown — all anxious to get to the Louisville races."

Racing went bigtime in 1832 when Oakland Racecourse opened southwest of Louisville. Oakland, with its elegant two-story clubhouse, was built on land local businessmen bought from Samuel Churchill, father of the Churchill brothers who figured so prominently in Louisville racing history half a century later. Samuel was president of the Louisville Association for the Improvement of the Breed of Horses, the group that owned Oaklawn. The 1839 nationally-advertised Wagner and Grey Eagle match race — a $14,000 winner-take-all event — attracted sportsmen from "the Bench, the Bar, the Senate and the Press." But Oakland was too far out in the country to attract spectators from Louisville and the track died a slow death, done in by its location and the financial Panic of 1857.

A year before the Civil War began, Louisvillians built Oakland's replacement, Woodlawn Race Course, in the midst of potato farms northeast of Louisville. Woodlawn was not as lavish as Oakland, and just as remote. The track opened the same afternoon a freak tornado uprooted trees, stopping the train that delivered passengers to Woodlawn's front gate. A cemetery for jockeys, located on the Westport Road corner of the property, gave credence to the description of a racing surface that was poorly harrowed and deceptively deep. The ill-fated riders were buried within sight of the track where they died.

Races were held at Woodlawn all during the Civil War, but, without restaurants or hotels nearby, Woodlawn couldn't compete when racing spread to cities nationwide after the war. By 1871, railroad politics forced Woodlawn to close. The much-advertised "Great

Bankrupt Sale of Woodlawn Subdivision" was held in June 1872.

Woodlawn did offer an enormous challenge trophy for which Woodford County horseman Robert A. Alexander paid Tiffany's $1,000. After Woodlawn closed, the trophy was turned over to the Louisville Jockey Club. Today, the Woodlawn vase is the perpetual trophy for the Preakness. The winner no longer takes possession of the well-insured, three-foot-tall, tiered silver "vahse" for a year, but gets a half-size replica which is challenge enough to polish!

In order to avoid military occupation or takeover of the L&N by Federal troops, Kentucky maintained a precarious balance between the North and the Confederacy during the war. Louisvillians were against secession; the most concentrated pocket of Confederate sympathizers was in Lexington, home of daring guerrilla leader John Hunt Morgan and his Hunt relations, who devoted their lives and fortunes to the South.

Louisville had no interest in territorial disputes or the slavery issue. The city's primary concern was how the hostilities affected L&N Railroad operations and profits. In 1859, Albert Fink, the railroad's chief engineer, supervised construction of the L&N road to Nashville. Then he designed and built the first Fink truss bridge, a span strong enough to bear the weight of a locomotive, across the Green River, west of Munfordville, extending L&N service southward through Bowling Green. When the line was completed, Louisville businessmen began to exert pressure on Nashville. Because of its considerable clout, the L&N controlled Bluegrass commerce as well.

After the Civil War, Nashville and the Bluegrass were the most important Thoroughbred breeding centers in the United States. By regulating shipping rates and transfer charges, the L&N was able to bleed them dry. Cincinnati businessmen, tired of paying exorbitant rates and getting poor service to boot, determined to build their own line south to Tennessee — one that bypassed the L&N and connected Lexington directly to Cincinnati. In 1869, Bluegrass farmers and merchants started lobbying the legislature on behalf of the Cincinnati railroad they saw as their deliverance from, and revenge on, the L&N.

Louisville businesses severed their northern ties after the Civil War, since the only market for Louisville-made farm tools and food staples was in the war-ravaged South. Former Confederate officers and soldiers became precious commodities when the city's Board of

Trade began promoting Louisville as the "Gateway to the South." These men urged the L&N to investigate customer complaints with "kindly feeling in a spirit of compromise and conciliation," but L&N management viewed "compromise" — decreasing their rates — as a threat to company profits and went on the offensive, calling Cincinnati merchants an "ingenious set of Yankee plodders and plotters, who propose to swarm upon the Southern country like ducks upon June-bugs and appropriate it to their own uses."

The two cities locked horns when Cincinnati petitioned the Tennessee Legislature for permission to build a track to Chattanooga. Just weeks after legislators denied Cincinnati's request, they approved a right-of-way for an L&N-Chattanooga line instead. With that, the long-simmering railroad war came to a boil. *The Cincinnati Commercial* promised readers that if the Cincinnati Southern's efforts were permanently thwarted, there would be a "small-sized rebellion in the South against the old dotards who allow themselves to be led by the nose by the selfish city of Louisville."

Almost overnight, the railroad issue became an all-out trade war, pitting Louisville against the Bluegrass. "Every day the people of Kentucky feel the L&N's iron heel upon them and upon their commerce," the *Cincinnati Commercial* told its disgruntled Lexington readership. Both Louisville's and Cincinnati's leaders entertained Kentucky legislators lavishly as they prepared to vote on the Ohio city's request for a right-of-way through central Kentucky. Louisville-based *Courier-Journal* editor, Henry Watterson, accused Kentucky lawmakers of taking bribes from Cincinnati officials. The only way the legislators could prove it wasn't true, Watterson reasoned, was to defeat the Yankee interloper, which is exactly what the Legislature did the first two times they voted. Bluegrass businessmen and farmers then boycotted Louisville goods and L&N service. By April of 1870, Louisville salesmen were no longer welcome in Lexington, Paris, Georgetown, Versailles or Danville. They "might as well go to Africa for orders," they were told.

No Thoroughbreds showed up at Woodlawn as trade with the Bluegrass dried up. Two thousand delegates attended a railroad convention that met in Lexington the following October. Marked for defeat in the upcoming elections were Western Kentucky representatives who sided with the L&N. Cincinnati Southern Railway backers introduced a third bill in January 1872, and this time, guided through the legislature by former United States Vice-President and

Confederate Gen. John C. Breckinridge, it won easily in the House and squeaked past the Senate by one vote. In spite of a major economic depression, construction of the line began in 1873. Cincinnati's Southern Railway reached Chattanooga in 1880. By then, Louisville's worst fears had been realized — goods from the Bluegrass were bypassing the city. Louisville's monopoly as a transportation crossroads was gone. The "iron horse" had finally been curbed.

Courting Southerners became the name of the game. It was time to cultivate magnolias and sing "Dixie" louder than it had ever been heard in Louisville before. From 1872 on, the Louisville Board of Trade lavished hospitality on Bluegrass businessmen, all part of a plan to woo them back to the river city. A new racetrack was a means to that end. The only racing in town was a sporadic meet or two held at Greenland, a poorly managed operation located south of the House of Refuge, near present-day Churchill Downs. Civic leaders, among them the Churchill brothers, got to work. The Louisville Jockey Club and Driving Park Association, eventually called Churchill Downs, opened three years later.

George Pullman built the first railroad sleeping car in 1865, making passenger transportation considerably more comfortable. As racetracks sprang up across the country, custom-fitted "horse cars" made horse transport equally luxurious. It was no accident that the Louisville Jockey Club was located within easy walking distance of the old L&N tracks and that L&N horsecar service to Bluegrass horse farms became the best in the business.

Whereas horse breeders had once been forced to limit their operations to sites along the L&N lines in Woodford County, completion of the Cincinnati-based line opened up land in Fayette and Bourbon Counties. As soon as the Cincinnati Southern Railway was operational, the flow of goods and horses northward from the Bluegrass was unstoppable. Kenton Countians, backed by Cincinnati businessmen, incorporated the Latonia Agricultural Association in 1881. On a 120-acre tract near Covington (across the Ohio River from Cincinnati) they built Latonia, a one-mile oval track, grandstand and clubhouse that opened for business in June 1883. Latonia took its name from the nearby resort, Lettonian Springs, a fashionable spa and site of informal race meets in the 1840s. Latonia was a handsome facility where attendance, fed by Cincinnati, frequently outstripped that of Churchill Downs. That meant more money for winners, so, for 20 years, Latonia, and the Latonia Derby, attracted better horses than the Kentucky Derby.

Latonia suffered from turn-of-the-century bookmaking scandals just as Churchill Downs did, but the Downs, ably directed by Matt Winn and backed by the clout of the still-mighty L&N, rebounded, becoming a major force in the racing industry by the end of World War I. In November 1918, Churchill Downs expanded, calling itself the Kentucky Jockey Club, Incorporated. The corporation managed four Kentucky tracks — Churchill, Douglas Park, Latonia and the Kentucky Association track in Lexington.

When Winn's Kentucky Jockey Club bought Latonia, it was the most profitable track in the state, attracting the best horses because of the purse structure. Then, in 1922, August Belmont, who was shepherding New York racing back into profitability, called Winn with a request. "We can't compete with Latonia," Winn recalled Belmont saying. "If you continue your liberality, all the horsemen will be deserting us and shipping to your track and there won't be much New York racing left." Winn, ever mindful of what New York meant to the Derby, discontinued Latonia's $10,000-to-$50,000 races, sacrificing the track to Eastern interests. Held in check, Latonia died a slow death.

Midway through the 1920s, Kentucky faced the Kentucky Anti-Race Track Gambling Commission's last onslaught. But thanks to a rousing speech by the Rev. Thomas Settle, an Episcopal priest newly come to Lexington from England, Commission efforts to shut down Thoroughbred racing were defeated by a single vote in the 1925 Legislature. As a reward for, and in honor of, Settle's eloquence, horsemen from around the country contributed at a fund with which Settle built the Church of the Good Shepherd, which stands near downtown Lexington today.

By 1929 the Kentucky Jockey Club had reorganized itself as the American Turf Association, adding to its holdings two Illinois tracks, Lincoln Fields and Washington Park, all under Matt Winn's dynamic leadership. Then, what anti-gambling zeal could not destroy, the Depression nearly did in. The American Turf Association was forced to sell its out-of-state tracks. The Kentucky Association track closed after the 1933 Spring Meet. The place was bankrupt, and about ready to fall down. For a community that had held two race meets every year since its founding — except in the spring of 1863 when Confederate General Kirby Smith camped on the track grounds — the loss was a blow to already financially-strapped Bluegrass horsemen.

In many ways, it was the best thing that ever happened to Kentucky's Thoroughbred industry. Lexington businessmen, eager to restore community values to racing, met for over a year before purchasing a portion of the Keeneland Stud as their new home. Keeneland, a horse farm located on the Versailles Road midway between Lexington and Versailles, next door to baking-powder heir Warren Wright's Calumet Farm, was thereby rescued from foreclosure and subsequently turned into the epitome of a traditional race course — as its owner J. O. (Jack) Keene had planned before he lost his fortune. When Keeneland opened, the old monogrammed Kentucky Association gateposts stood at the entrance to the parklike site, which to this day has no public address system — all the better to remind visitors that racing should be observed, not shouted.

On October 15, 1936, Keeneland conducted the first nine-day meet on its new mile-and-a-quarter course. "Racing as it was meant to be" has always been Keeneland's motto. "We want a place where those who love horses can come and picnic with us. We are not running a race plant to hear the click of the mutuel machines. We don't care if the people who come here bet or not. If they want to bet there is a place for them to do it. But we want them to come out here to enjoy God's sunshine, the fresh air and to watch horses race," Keeneland Board member Hal Price Headley told the press in 1937. A photo-finish camera wasn't installed at Keeneland until 1946.

There was no group of die-hard horsemen at hand to rescue Latonia the way Lexingtonians rescued Bluegrass racing. The American Turf Association, by then a shadow of its former self, shut down Latonia in 1937. Some claimed, with good reason, that Winn had no use for a track in Northern Kentucky competing for the few stables still racing horses during the Depression. The site was sold to Standard Oil of Ohio when the United States entered World War II. Today, Latonia is a shopping center on the outskirts of Covington. Racing in Northern Kentucky did not resume until 1959.

During the war, the United States depended on the railroads to move equipment and personnel. Shipping Thoroughbreds to racetracks or yearling sales at Saratoga, N. Y., and then providing passenger service for spectators and buyers, was not deemed essential to the war effort, except at Churchill Downs. Keeneland closed; its three wartime Spring Meets were held at the Louisville track, which, thanks to Winn's creativity, operated throughout the war. Keeneland reopened early in April 1946, on a wet, foggy day, when the tote board in the infield didn't work and spectators couldn't see the horses, but nothing dampened the spirits of the 10,000 attendees.

In Keeneland's 50th-anniversary book, board chairman James E. "Ted" Bassett III quoted T. S. Eliot, "Tradition cannot be inherited, and if you want it you must obtain it by great labor." In 1986 it could be said of every Kentucky-bred person on Keeneland's Board that he or she knew how to saddle and bridle a horse and, if necessary, to clean and re-bed a stall. Today, the Keeneland Library contains the most complete collection of Thoroughbred history and statistics available to the public. The non-dividend-paying Keeneland Association has long been the largest single corporate donor — $6.9 million to date — to community programs, health services and educational institutions in the Bluegrass.

"Keeneland is extremely pleased to share the success of its Thoroughbred racing and sales with the citizens of the city and state," is how Keeneland president Bill Greely prefaced his announcement of gifts totaling $322,135 distributed among 53 organizations in December 1994. Keeneland's Thoroughbred auctions — source of Keeneland's wealth — attract buyers from around the world. At the 1985 Summer Select Sales, a colt bred by Churchill's board chairman, Warner L. Jones, sold to English soccer-pools bookmaker baron Robert Sangster for a record-breaking $13.1 million. During the high-rolling '80s, jets lined up on the tarmac at Bluegrass Airport, across the Versailles Road from Keeneland, looked like a miniature United Nations assemblage, poised to transport men and horses around the world.

When England's Queen Elizabeth II visited Bluegrass horse farms in 1984, Keeneland made no special preparations for her arrival other than creating a mile-and-an-eighth challenge cup turf race in her honor. It is the only racetrack in America where spectators can visit the stable area of the beautifully planted, meandering site without a racing commission's license. Staff are at hand to graciously rescue those who get lost in the maze of barns. Change at Keeneland comes only with community backing and approval. Sunday racing was inaugurated at the Spring Meet in 1991, the same year a charming gift shop opened on the grounds.

Kentucky's newest competitive track is Turfway Park, a renovation of the New Latonia track that opened in Florence, Ky., 10 miles south of Cincinnati, in 1959. New Latonia was dogged by administration problems that eventually drove it into the ground. By the time real estate developer Jerry L. Carroll bought New Latonia for $125 million in 1986, the tote board was being propped up with two-by-fours and the facility was a sorry sight. Twenty million dollars worth of improvements later, Turfway has been recognized as the fastest-growing track in America.

Stricter tax laws brought an end to hobby racing and turned the last decade into a bumpy road for horse-farm owners, throwing well-known establishments such as Calumet and Spendthrift into bankruptcy after improvident heirs, with their legions of lawyers and consultants, flew too high. No more sales records are being broken at Keeneland today.

Tracks, regardless of their philosophy about racing, must make it worthwhile for horsemen to be there. Kentucky purses still rank behind California's, but the natural advantages of raising and racing horses in the Bluegrass keeps top trainers here year after year. At the heart of Kentucky's industry are still the careful, experienced Thoroughbred breeders and owners, individuals not overwhelmed by the combination of science, art, determination and luck that racing requires.

**M. Lewis Clark and his children, c. 1854
Lutie Clark is at right.**

Chapter Four

Churchill's First Colonel

Even today, almost a century after his death, everything about Meriwether Lewis Clark, Jr., seems larger than life. His family connections were the oldest; his ancestors, national heroes; his lifestyle so flamboyant that the Kentucky Derby he created has come to be America's best-known race.

Clark's grandfather was Gen. William Clark, Lewis and Clark Expedition co-leader, afterwards governor of Missouri. Louisville's founder, George Rogers Clark, was Clark's great-uncle. Gen. Clark sent his son, the senior Meriwether Lewis Clark, to West Point, where one of his classmates was Richard Ten Broeck, later a prominent figure in 19th-Century racing circles, as well as a relative by marriage of Meriwether Lewis Clark, Jr. Ten Broeck was kicked out of West Point for insubordination and drunkenness; the general's son earned his commission as an engineer, and served in both the Mexican War and the Civil War.

Clark's marriage to Abigail Prather Churchill linked him to one of Kentucky's first families. Like the Clarks, the Churchills were Virginia-born merchants and land-owners. They came to Jefferson County in 1785 and bought 300 acres of land south of Louisville that today includes Audubon Park, the Eastern Parkway-Preston Highway interchange, parts of the University of Louisville campus and Churchill Downs.

M. Lewis Clark, Jr., nicknamed "Lutie," was born at Spring Grove, the plantation home of his maternal grandparents, Samuel and Abigail Oldham Churchill. When Lutie was still an infant, during the spring of 1846, Abigail Churchill Clark returned to St. Louis with her four children while her husband went off to the Mexican War. Clark may have been a war hero, one descendant wrote, but he badly neglected his ever-growing family.

After Abigail died, following the birth of their seventh child, Clark parcelled his children out among Churchill kin. Lutie was sent to Spring Grove. When his grandmother died a year later, he was first passed along to his aunt, Emily Zane, then to her unmarried brothers, John and Henry Churchill, to raise. The Churchill boys, as

Louisvillians called them, had inherited the lion's share of the Churchill property. With the income from their well-invested fortune, they were gentlemen who had no need to work. Lutie was doted on by his uncles and the dignified Black couple who ran the Sixth Street Churchill household.

Then, early in 1858, John, almost 40, married a widow 11 years his junior. When their son, William Henry, was born within the year, Lutie was displaced as the favored Churchill heir. Mrs. Churchill died a week before her first wedding anniversary. The baby died nine months later. For Lutie at least, life returned to normal. He attended St. Joseph's College at Bardstown, Ky., where he was an indifferent student. Unlike his father, who served under Lee through Appomattox, Lutie skipped the Civil War. He looked a lot like his uncles — tall, lean, muscular and mustached. From them, he inherited his taste for custom-made suits, good food and champagne. The Churchills raced a small stable of Thoroughbreds — their father had been the first president of the Oaklawn Race Course in the 1830s. Lutie sat beside his uncles at Woodlawn Race Course and Greeneland; racing was what he loved best. His job as an assistant bank cashier, within walking distance of home, was not a demanding one. In 1867 his uncles sent him on a "Grand Tour" of Europe. A Churchill family friend, Confederate Gen. William Preston, wrote his former comrade-in-arms, still-exiled Gen. John C. Breckinridge about Lutie: "My kinsman, Mr. M. L. Clark is going in a fortnight to Europe, to remain for a few months. He is a young gentleman of high character and intelligence, for whom I have a strong regard." It was the best introduction to England and Thoroughbred racing Lutie could have wanted.

While still in Washington, before siding with the South, John C. Breckinridge had been president of the Kentucky Association for the Improvement of the Breed of Horses. He actively promoted Lexington racing and became an avid racing fan in Great Britain, where he was highly regarded for his cultured ways and leadership of the Orphan Brigade, the Kentucky unit that played such a passionate, devil-may-care role in Confederate Army history. Less than five years later, Breckinridge had a profound effect on the development of racing in Louisville.

When Lutie got back from Europe, he switched from banking to the tobacco business, a job his uncles no doubt secured for him. In 1871 he eloped with Mary Martin Anderson, whose aunt was the wife of Lutie's father's classmate, Richard Ten Broeck. The eccentric Ten Broeck, whose Hurstbourne Stud was located in eastern Jefferson County, had, by then, an international reputation as a brilliant horseman and reckless gambler. Marriage to Mrs. Ten Broeck's niece gave Lutie Clark entree to English racing circles as well as a link to Ten Broeck, who owned several Southern tracks.

Later that same year, Lutie's 57-year-old Uncle William married Katherine Clark, a 35-year-old cousin. She died in the fall of 1872, after less than a year of marriage. Lutie was now heir-apparent to two widower uncles, and his second European trip, bankrolled by his uncles, was in the planning stage. Clark's job was to bring back plans for a new racing concept, one that would entice Bluegrass owners to send their horses to Louisville. During his stay in England, Clark was the guest of Admiral Rous, English racing's "Dictator," a man who believed that every aspect of racing should be honest and aboveboard.

Late in 1873, Clark came home with ideas about how to build a racetrack and eliminate bookmaking by using French pari-mutuel wagering machines. In spite of hard times, plans for the Churchill-backed venture went forward. Uncle John was the track's first treasurer. Uncle Henry was on the board. This was no hobby horse the Churchills were riding; there was too much at stake.

In the summer of 1869, General Breckinridge, taking advantage of the general amnesty offered Confederate soldiers, returned to Lexington and was appointed general counsel to the newly-proposed Cincinnati Southern Railway. He was also vice-president of the Elizabethtown, Lexington & Big Sandy Railroad, overseeing its construction and operation until the Panic of 1873 shut it down. Breckinridge's work on behalf of the Cincinnati Southern Railway brought him in contact with Lutie Clark once again.

Louisville vehemently opposed the Cincinnati line, since it would free the Bluegrass from L&N Railroad domination and break the L&N's hold on the lucrative Southern trade. Newspaper editor Henry Watterson, an overbearing "Southern gentleman," asked Lexingtonians if they wanted to be associated with Yankees. Better to live with Yankees, they replied, than to die at the hands of the L&N!

Once Breckinridge espoused the cause, even the blustering Watterson knew the Bluegrass would win. The 1873 Legislature, faced with bribes and Breckinridge, accepted the bribes, then voted for the Cincinnati plan. The Ohio route, when completed, would serve Lexington directly, taking produce and horses into Cincinnati, Louisville's prime competitor for the rich river trade. One way or another, Bluegrass business had to be lured back to Louisville.

Thoroughbred owners needed a track to showcase their racing stock, especially after the 1873 Panic further depressed already low yearling prices. What better place to build one than on damp, crawfish-ridden Churchill land, next to the L&N tracks? The Churchill brothers, not Lutie Clark, were the entrepreneurs who put the Louisville Jockey Club and Driving Park Association together, with young Lutie acting as president and on-site manager. Half the Louisville Jockey Club board members were local bankers, hotel men and streetcar company owners, in whose businesses the Churchills held stock. The other half were men like John Wesley Hunt Reynolds, Bluegrass Thoroughbred owners with sizeable farms and whiskey interests. Reynolds was the cousin of dead Confederate leader John Hunt Morgan. Reynolds' uncle was Thomas Hunt, a fellow officer in Breckinridge's Orphan Brigade. Horse racing, like Kentucky politics, had a way of making strange bedfellows.

By selling 320 shares of stock at $100 a share, the Louisville Jockey Club came up with $32,000 to build a racetrack. In June 1874, Clark announced plans for the track. In spring and fall the facility would be devoted to racing, but otherwise, Clark stated, people were welcome to use the grounds for carriage driving — hence the awkward and lengthy name.

Noted architect John Andrewartha was retained to design the grandstand and Jockey Club headquarters. Located on the first turn — as far away from the stable area as possible — this rustic two-story retreat, for Jockey Club members and their guests, had a kitchen and a "water closet," the only indoor toilet within miles. Both buildings were on the east side of the track, situated so that they faced the afternoon sun.

Andrewartha was then designing the *Courier-Journal* building. He submitted sketchy plans that a long-suffering carpenter's crew none too successfully worked out for themselves. Investors' money ran out before the grandstand was begun, so Clark borrowed money to build a simple, flat-roofed structure. When final costs ran way over estimate, the Louisville Jockey Club refused to pay for the work, claiming the clubhouse roof leaked. The builder protested that he had followed Andrewartha's sketches for the canted, asphalt-covered roof as best he could, but he was finally forced to file suit to recover his costs.

In August 1874, a son, John Henry Churchill, nicknamed "Churchill," was born to the Clarks. Daughters followed in 1876 and 1878. By then, Lutie Clark was too involved in the realization of his dream to give his family much notice.

The track opened amid great hoopla on May 17, 1875. The dirt road from Third Street had been widened and watered, the lawn around the clubhouse had been sodded and there were stalls for 150 horses. Local newspaper headlines that week told of the exploits of outlaws Frank and Jesse James; the auction of an eastern Jefferson County tract, Crescent Hill, site of a defunct racetrack associated with the Southwestern Agricultural Association; and, lastly, 54-year-old John C. Breckinridge's death, hours after the first Derby was run. Except for Greeneland, the Louisville Jockey Club had no competition in Jefferson County.

The Kentucky Derby was not planned as the main attraction of the inaugural meet, but when H. P. McGrath's Aristides set a new world's record for the mile-and-a-half distance on opening day, the crowd went wild. Racing three-year-olds was relatively new. Heretofore the public had preferred betting on seasoned favorites. For that reason, Clark commissioned a gigantic trophy for the Louisville Cup, a highly publicized handicap race for older horses, run mid-meet. The trophy was a huge, downright ugly piece of Victorian silver — replete with solid silver horsehead handles. The winner, Ballankeel, was allowed to drink out of it after the presentation! The whereabouts of this $1,000 watering trough have long been forgotten — the race itself lapsed after 1887 — but Ballankeel's jockey, William Walker, went on to become one of the great names in American racing, and, three years later, a considerable thorn in Clark's ever-expanding side.

The only other trophy at the inaugural meet was a silver bowl awarded to the winner of the Gentleman's Cup Race, in which a member of a recognized jockey club rode his own horse. Three men entered, but the South Carolina Jockey Club's Calhoun Smith opted not to brave the rain and sloppy track. The race was won by Louisville Jockey Club member A. Trigg Moss. At the presentation, Clark filled the trophy with champagne and poured it over the already-drenched Moss' head. Sadly, this gentleman's cup has also been lost to time. By the end of the Spring Meet, 29-year-old Lutie was hailed as an entrepreneurial success, the head of an up-and-coming local business. It didn't matter that the track made no profit the first year. Racetracks seldom did.

Fame transformed Lutie into "Colonel" Clark, an honorary title that went with his new-found status. "Colonel" Clark probably thought little about his Uncle Henry's second marriage in 1876, two months after an overconfident Thoroughbred owner, Col. George A. Custer, gained lasting fame in a valley along the Little Big Horn River in the Montana Territory. Churchills always favored male heirs over wives and daughters. Henry's bride was widowed, childless Julia Prentiss. She was 34 years younger than her 62-year-old husband, whom Lutie correctly reckoned was too old to father a child.

Clark had little time to dwell on family matters. His job entailed not only managing the Louisville Jockey Club's annual meets, but traveling around the Southern racing circuit, acting as a steward while drumming up business for his track. In 1878, a winning pari-mutuel ticket on Derby victor Day Star paid a whopping $30.60, but racing's real stars that spring were Ten Broeck, equine hero of the Bluegrass, and "darling Mollie McCarthy," the West Coast champion. The two took a "friendly stroll" in front of the grandstand the last day of the Spring Meet. Clark had already booked a Ten Broeck-Mollie McCarthy match race for the Fourth of July.

Ten Broeck was owned by Midway, Ky., breeder Frank B. Harper. Ten Broeck's trainer, "Rolly" Colston, had been a well-known jockey. Fillies seldom raced against stallions, but Mollie seemed good enough to beat eight-year-old Ten Broeck, which had finished fifth in the 1875 Derby. After Ten Broeck won the hot, humid Independence Day match race handily, there were unsettling reports in *The Thoroughbred Record* about Clark. Prior to race time, as rumors of race-fixing and dirty tricks ran rampant, Clark set up track patrols and policemen to guard Ten Broeck's stall, then threatened to lynch William Walker, Ten Broeck's jockey, if he, Clark, found any evidence of cheating. The race was a fizzle the exhausted Mollie didn't even finish. For several hours after the race, Clark was unconscious, reportedly suffering from sunstroke.

Two weeks later, Walker told a correspondent from *The Cincinnati Enquirer* all about Clark's bizarre behavior when the reporter, who was delighted to discredit Clark and Louisville any way he could, visited Frank Harper's farm. Angry Bluegrass horsemen, all Walker's clients, snubbed Clark. He never picked a fight with Lexington again.

In 1881, the senior Clark committed suicide at the home of J.

Stoddard Johnson, a prominent Frankfort lawyer and Clark's former Confederate comrade-in-arms, whose permanent house guest Clark and his second wife had become. Lutie handled all the funeral details, burying his father in the family plot at Cave Hill Cemetery.

For the next 15 years, young Clark's pompousness and weight grew apace. Because of his height he had always been a standout in any crowd; in the course of entertaining colleagues he became a standout because of his enormous girth as well. As racing consumed his life, Clark became a father like his own father, never home long enough to figure in the lives of his wife and three children. He had long since fallen in love with racetracks and there was no way his wife could compete. The Clarks separated. By 1886, Mary Clark and the children were living with widower John Churchill.

Lutie stayed at the newly-formed Pendennis Club, the private gentlemen's retreat which his uncles had helped found. From there, every spring and fall during the 1880s, he led the way to Churchill Downs, driving the stylish red Louisville Jockey Club tallyho pulled by four high-stepping bays. The cream of Louisville society followed him. Hotel and restaurant business peaked at Derby, which was then run in the middle of May. To accommodate tourists, theater-owners booked the biggest names they could get. In return, celebrities became part of the "Derby crowd."

The most famous was Polish actress Helena Modjeska, for whom local confectioner Anton Busath named a pillow-shaped caramel-covered candy. In 1883, Modjeska and her husband, a Polish count, were Clark's Derby guests, accompanying him to the Jockey Clubhouse lawn where a sumptuous Derby brunch awaited them. Part of the day's ritual was the preparation of a quart-sized silver loving cup filled with mint julep, the potent iced bourbon and sugarwater drink beloved of Southerners. Clark's brew was meant to be passed from guest to guest, so each one could toast the Derby with a hearty draught. As guest of honor, Modjeska was handed the cup first. She took one sip; then a swallow. To the amazement of the other guests, she drained the container, finally asking Clark, in her heavily accented voice, to "please fix one for the Count." Clark was glad to oblige.

As the Louisville Jockey Club's presiding steward, the 300-pound Clark was a sight to see, binoculars in hand, monitoring every race from the judges' stand, dressed in custom-tailored suits and pale yellow kid gloves, with a flower in his lapel. He had a taste for fine wine and champagne and entertained business associates lavishly in the city's best restaurants. Reporters began to write about how ruddy his complexion became when he hefted himself up the stairs and into the judges' box after a night on the town.

Those who had no reason to cross Clark called him a bastion of propriety, good for racing. To his credit, he brought the first pari-mutuel wagering machines into Kentucky and tried, without success, to get the public to use them. He presided over the first American Turf Congress, held at Louisville's Galt House Hotel, and wrote racing rules that are still in force today. He worked for a uniform system of weights and pioneered the stakes system, creating the Great American Stallion Stake, on which the present-day Breeders' Cup is modeled. Clark spoke out against betting by officials and reporters, which certainly didn't endear him to the press. His only Derby wager, he bragged, was the price of a new hat.

Like Admiral Rous and other old-time horsemen, Clark discouraged the racing of two-year-olds, no matter how short the distance. His fight against bookmakers, whom he blamed for sullying racing's good name, was unending. Supporters described Clark as a law unto himself, absolutely impartial in his racing decisions, a man no one could bully or outwit. Left unsaid was the fact that Clark was becoming something of a bully himself. It once came close to costing him his life.

In 1879, Clark refused prominent Crab Orchard breeder T. G. Moore permission to race at the Louisville Jockey Club. Clark claimed Moore's entry fees were past due. Moore had been a stalwart on the Kentucky racing circuit since before the Civil War. He took Clark's pronouncement as the personal insult that it was and demanded an apology. The Colonel refused and ordered Moore out of his Galt House office. When Moore told Clark he would bear the consequences of his decision not to apologize, Clark knocked Moore to the ground, held a gun on him and ordered him off the premises. Moore left the room, got a gun and shot Clark through the door. The bullet hit Clark in the chest, lodging under his right arm. Moore turned himself in at the police station, but no charges were brought. He was subsequently ruled off the track, not because of the shooting incident, but because of the dispute over the fees. Clark, to his credit, reversed the decision a year later.

During the 1880s, Clark's reputation as an arrogant, quick-tempered man nobody dared cross, grew. He was not well-liked by locals, who took to calling the track "Churchill's downs," a reference to English racing that poked fun at the highfalutin president, as well as reminding him who really controlled the Louisville Jockey Club's purse strings. In 1883 the local press picked up the nickname, which has since become the track's incorporated, trademarked name.

It was the age of the bookmaker. Clark's pari-mutuel machines were discarded while pool halls and betting parlors flourished, as did grass-roots citizens' groups opposed to gambling. Through it all, Clark continued to live high on the hog, hobnobbing with the rich and famous wherever he traveled. His uncles were growing old. Probably he planned to recoup his fortune, and a great deal more, at their deaths. Newspapers reported rumors of Clark demanding cases of wine, above and beyond the fees set for his services as a steward. The rumors were fueled by the terms of an 1883 stakes race, named the Moet & Chandon, after an expensive French champagne Clark fancied. The winner had to provide the Jockey Club with four cases of Moet & Chandon, which reporters and Jockey Club members drank right after the race. The "gift" cost more than the $1,000 the track added to the $100 entry fee each owner put into the stakes pot. The Moet & Chandon Stakes was discontinued after 1887. Few owners could afford the price of victory!

Clark's 1889 post-Derby party at the Pendennis Club was one of the most lavish ever held there. The layout of the Downs, including the chute for dash racing, was reproduced in miniature in the center of the host's table. Thus the Derby could be re-run by guests who had wagered heavily on Proctor Knott, the popular Tennessee horse named for a former Kentucky governor — only to see Spokane, the interloper from Montana, win. It had been a great day and a great race. It was the end of a decade, and Clark's last good year.

The Moore incident wasn't the only disagreement Clark settled with a gun. Clark was working as a $100-a-day steward at Garfield Park when a bartender at his hotel took offense at Clark's calling Chicagoans "thieves and liars," and told Clark so. Clark vanished, then reappeared with a gun. Resting the muzzle on the bartender's chest, Clark forced the man to apologize. There were witnesses, because *The Chicago Post* carried a detailed account of the episode, which *The LOUISVILLE COMMERCIAL* gleefully reprinted. The Churchill brothers could not have been pleased with the publicity.

Later came the report of a shooting and a scuffle at Garfield Park. Clark, the steward there, was arrested and taken off to jail in a paddy wagon with a burly Black policeman seated on top of him to hold him down. Life in Chicago was every bit as tough as racing in Louisville had become!

In November 1890, John Churchill, 71 and a widower for 30 years, remarried. His wife was 36-year-old Tina Nicholas, from a Kentucky family as distinguished as the Churchills. Although John and Tina were not blood relatives, they were certainly, through family connections, kissin' cousins. As with Diomed a century before, the marriage gave John new vigor. Their son, John Rowan Pope Churchill, Jr., was born 10 months later.

Long-suffering Mary Clark could take no more of Louisville. In January 1891 there was a note in *THE CRITIC*: "Mrs. Mary Clark is completing arrangements for a prolonged visit to Europe, where she will probably make her home for many years." John, with whom she and her children lived, probably made her a settlement that gave her a life of her own. There is no mention of her ever divorcing Clark; she returned to Louisville only once, for her daughter's coming-out party, living with John and Tina for almost a year. The 1898 city directory listed her as "removed to Paris, France," where she remained until her death.

The same newspaper that reported Mary Clark's leavetaking had no great fondness for her husband or Charles D. Jacob, the far-sighted civic leader who was four times Mayor of Louisville. In the summer of 1889, Jacob made Clark park commissioner at a reported salary of $6,000 a year. Clark had bigger ideas about the expansion of Southern Parkway than *THE CRITIC* liked. The short-lived job provided Clark with sorely-needed cash and a way to start widening the route to the Downs. It left the city fathers with a $20,000 bill they were totally unprepared to pay!

As early as 1884, the Churchills began writing wills. Henry's first will left Julia the family home, $60,000 and $800 yearly rent from the track. In 1889, two years before he died, Henry rewrote his will, leaving his entire estate to his wife. By mutual agreement, the Louisville Jockey Club land became John's property. Clark wasn't even mentioned in the will. Had John not married in 1890, Clark might have inherited the land the track was on. The birth of a healthy Churchill heir must have been a distinct shock to the already intemperate Clark.

The following year, John Churchill wrote his will. His wife, Tina, was named administrator. She and their son got everything, except for 46 acres allotted to Clark and his three children. Clark was to choose the best land from property adjoining the Louisville Jockey Club grounds, but John made it very clear that Clark was to have no part of the track itself. In an 1896 codicil, John specified the land Clark and his three children were to get and left his widowed sister money he had once earmarked for Clark's children. Lutie, it would appear, had tested his uncle's patience once too often. By the time John died in 1897, Clark was serving as a steward at Churchill Downs. From time to time he listed his residence as the Jockey Clubhouse — quite a comedown from palatial Chicago hotels and Louisville's Pendennis Club.

No doubt Clark, who did his gambling on the stock market, lost heavily in 1893 when the overheated economy exploded and the New York Stock Exchange closed its doors for 10 days. The 1893 Panic threw thousands out of work, causing the first of two severe nationwide economic depressions in the 1890s. At the center of this disaster were Astors, Belmonts, Keenes, Fisks and Goulds — "gentlemen" who shortly thereafter created the exclusive New York Jockey Club to keep racing pure and untainted.

Late in the summer of 1894, Clark gave up. The Louisville Jockey Club went through virtual bankruptcy and a total change of command. Shortly after the takeover, as a new double-steepled grandstand took shape, *THE LOUISVILLE COMMERCIAL* referred to the track as "Church Hill Downs." It had been purchased by bookmakers who styled themselves the New Louisville Jockey Club. They ran the Downs for the next eight years, discontinuing the money-losing Fall Meets after 1895.

What the Churchills had invested in the track was a pittance compared to their combined fortunes, estimated at $750,000 when John's will was read. That they would no longer come to their nephew's aid, or bail out the racetrack, says a great deal about how strained family relationships had become.

The new owners took over the Churchill land lease agreement and built a twin-spired wooden grandstand on the west side of the track from plans drawn by Louisvillian Joseph D. Baldez — a 24-year-old draftsman with the firm of D. X. Murphy & Bro. There was no clubhouse for members, or separate seating for the ladies, but there was a brand new, 60-foot wide, 200-foot long, brick-floored betting enclosure only a stone's throw from the new saddling paddock. The myth of racing as sport was replaced by the reality of a view-and-bet gambling operation. And officials had two centrally located surveillance towers from which they could oversee the entire operation.

For the last five years of his life Clark was a nomad, moving from track to track. His son worked at the L&N Railroad's Chicago office, so Clark sometimes called the Windy City his home. He traveled constantly; at one time or another he was presiding judge at Memphis, Nashville, Dallas, and Mexico City. Life must have been a constant strain for the grossly obese "Colonel" who was paid by the Association of Western Bookmakers to "enforce honest sport."

Then a second financial panic, set off by Wall Street stock manipulators, made Clark's professional life more precarious than ever in 1897, as tracks closed and Thoroughbreds were sold for horsemeat. With no prospects for a Churchill inheritance, Clark's financial position was bleak. He continued to speculate on the stock market, but he had none of his uncles' genius for investment. Toward the end he was living with Emily Zane, his first foster mother. What income Clark had, came from the $100 a day he earned as a steward. On April 22, 1899, Clark was in Memphis, officiating at the Spring Meet there. Afterwards, newspapers reported that he was in poor health from the time he arrived, suffering from nervous prostration and narcolepsy, barely able to get to and from the track each day. There was no question that his death was suicide; he sat on his bed, put a gun to his head and pulled the trigger.

In 1934, historian Rogers Clark Ballard Thruston, a relative of Clark's, reviewed all the records and wrote a descendant: "It looks to me as if his income was derived almost, if not exclusively, from his salary in judging the races. I doubt if he had any material income from invested capital. His memory was failing and my conclusion is that he possibly feared senility was coming on him, although he was then only 53 years of age. He realized that should senility overtake him, he would probably land in the poor house and die a pauper's death. Death was preferable."

Clark wrote no will. When his estate was probated, he had less than $3,000 in his bank account. Wine and liquor in storage, his only liquid assets, sold for $14,300. There may have been some truth to the rumors after all!

**Sallie Ward Lawrence painted by G. P. A. Healy, 1860
Collection of J. B. Speed Museum, Louisville, Kentucky**

Chapter Five

Mrs. Downs — The Belle of Louisville

From the 1840s until the end of the century, Louisvillians had two surefire topics of conversation — war and the Wards. Both made headlines regularly, especially Sallie, Louisville's brightest belle, the legend of loveliness, a social pioneer, trendsetter and, some said, the most beautiful woman who ever lived!

Sallie, like most people at the heart of Kentucky racing history, was a daughter of the Bluegrass. Sallie Johnson, the grandmother for whom she was named, was the daughter of pioneer Baptist politician Col. Robert Johnson, of Orange County, Va. Van Buren's vice-president, Richard Mentor Johnson, who claimed to have killed the great Indian leader Tecumseh in the War of 1812, was her grandmother's brother. The Johnson clan grew so quickly that Robert Johnson's great-grandson once remarked that he could ride for miles and never be out of sight of close relatives!

Grandmother Sallie Johnson married Col. William T. Ward, an Indian agent and early Georgetown, Ky., settler from Virginia who owned vast tracts of land in the South. Their sons were Junius Richard Ward and Robert Johnson Ward. Both chose wives from prestigious Bluegrass families. Junius married Matilda Viley, sister of a neighboring Scott County Thoroughbred breeder, Captain Willa Viley, and amassed a fortune in the cotton trade. When not in Georgetown, Ward and his family lived on his Lake Washington estate in Mississippi. In partnership with Viley, Gen. Abe Buford and Richard Ten Broeck, Ward bought Dr. Elisha Warfield's famous Thoroughbred, Lexington, and ran him in the Great State Stakes at New Orleans. It was Junius who built the fabulous Greek Revival mansion, Ward Hall, completed in 1856 and still standing near Georgetown.

In 1825, Robert, then a 27-year-old widower, married Emily Flournoy, 14-year-old daughter of Matthew Flournoy of Walnut Hall. Sallie, their oldest child, was born in 1827. Robert Ward, like his brother, was a businessmen. When Sallie was 10, he moved his family to Louisville. They lived in a well-staffed mansion at Second and Walnut that boasted its own conservatory, where German gardener Henry Nanz grew camellias and named a fragrant yellow rose he perfected in Sallie's honor. She was sent to Philadelphia for her schooling, and before she was 18, newspapers proclaimed her the belle of the state. She did outrageous things, such as riding pell-mell through the city market building, toppling bushels of produce and leaving a very frightened escort behind. All was forgiven the following day when she returned to pay for the damage she had done. The Ward children, Louisvillians claimed, weren't wild, merely high-spirited. The Johnsons weren't always so impressed with their Ward kin. One relative wrote another about the Ward escapades: "They have always considered gambling and unique gestures a virtue."

At the outbreak of the Mexican War in 1846, Sallie was color bearer at the sendoff for the troops. She so inspired Louisville's fighting men that the flag she presented to them was never lowered during battle and when they returned to Louisville, they marched to the Ward home and presented it back to her!

The year the war started, Sallie's younger sister married Collin Throckmorton, son of the owner of a highly successful local hotel called the Galt House. Three years later, Sallie married T. Bigelow Lawrence, scion of a very old and conservative Boston family. The groom's mother attended the lavish Louisville wedding dressed in a plain, dark cotton frock. It was prelude to disaster. As Mrs. Bigelow Lawrence, Sallie arrived in Boston on April Fool's Day, 1849. Her lifestyle — late to bed, late to rise and always a little devil-may-care — shocked her in-laws. When she wore strong perfume and rouged her cheeks in the morning — something no Boston lady ever did — her horrified mother-in-law took her to task. Sallie wrote home for advice. Emily Flournoy Ward wrote back: "Seem to obey, but do as you please. Defy your husband and stick to it with some of your mother's spunk."

Sallie did just that. At a formal reception for a visiting ambassador, she appeared in a simple gingham shift. When the Lawrences gave a ball in her honor, she made her grand entrance in a costume of white satin bloomers and jeweled Persian slippers. Boston party-goers were horrified to see a married woman, indeed any woman, so brazenly expose her legs! Mrs. Lawrence ordered her daughter-in-law to return to her room and change. Instead, Sallie started packing and wrote her father to come get her. After four months of marriage, she headed back to Louisville — ostensibly for a short visit — taking her entire wardrobe of 80 gowns with her!

Family and friends welcomed Sallie with open arms. The

harsh Boston climate, they agreed, was bad for her health. Her father wrote Bigelow Lawrence, suggesting he take up residence in Louisville. Lawrence refused, and, in a total lapse of manners, published a pamphlet about Sallie's behavior, which he circulated in Boston. "We will not say," he wrote, "what motives wedded her so closely to Louisville. . . We will not say whether other reasons than those that lie on the surface bore her to Louisville and bound her there."

Kentuckians were horrified. Gentlemen did not air marital differences in writing or condemn their wives by innuendo, especially wives related to some of the most prominent politicians in the Bluegrass. In short order, a sympathetic Kentucky Legislature granted Sallie a divorce and her parents threw a fancy dress ball for her. Among the eligible bachelors who attended were the Churchill brothers and G. F. Downs. Sallie was in the marriage market again!

In 1851 she married her father's business partner, distinguished, wealthy Lexingtonian Dr. Robert P. Hunt. Because she was a divorcee, his family opposed the match on religious grounds, saying it would doom Hunt to Hell. The wedding was a quiet one, to which they were not invited. He wrote them afterwards, "I would far rather go to Hell with Sallie Ward than to Heaven without her." The Hunts moved to New Orleans, where they entertained lavishly when not traveling abroad. Sallie Ward Lawrence Hunt was the toast of the town.

Two years later, tragedy struck. Sallie's brother, Matt, a scholar and poet, murdered Professor William H. G. Butler, popular young principal of the school their younger brother Will attended. The facts were undisputed. Butler had punished the boy for misbehaving with five or six licks of a leather strap. Matt bought a gun, went to the school the next morning and shot Butler point-blank in the chest. He died an agonizingly slow death, leaving behind a young wife and infant son.

Louisvillians were outraged by the senseless crime. Ward's attorneys, claiming he couldn't get justice at home, had the trial moved to Hardin County, where a sympathetic, well-bribed jury acquitted Ward. When the news reached Louisville, an enraged mob tried to burn the Ward mansion, but that wasn't the worst of the Ward family's problems. A week later, Matt eloped with Anna Key, the Hardin County jailer's daughter, and arrangements had to be made for Matt to take his pregnant and very socially unacceptable bride to a plantation the Wards owned in Arkansas.

Neither the murder nor the marriage tarnished Sallie's reputation. She traveled between New Orleans and Louisville, regularly visiting Ward Hall, where she played hostess for her widowed uncle Junius. The Belle of Louisville set fashion standards in the South. Parisian designers vied for the privilege of dressing her. She once wore a gown adorned with real roses, to which diamonds, sparkling like dew, had been affixed. Society editors recorded her every move. The Sallie Ward slipper and the Sallie Ward walk (an undulating gait) were headlined from Virginia to Louisiana. In the glitter of the 1850s, Sallie was a bright and shining star.

She loved racing. When her uncle's horse Lexington won the Great State Stakes at the Metairie Course in 1854, she was there in all her glory. Old General Ward had once named a promising filly after his enchanting granddaughter. If a Thoroughbred was particularly beautiful, it was called a Sallie Ward. The *American Stud Book* lists four horses registered by that name, including an 1851 filly named Sallie Ward Jr. for her dam, Sallie Ward. Sallie herself knew fine bloodstock when she saw it. She wagered, not for money, but for gloves — fine imported kid gloves — a dozen pairs at a time. Between partying and traveling, she bore Dr. Hunt three children, but only a son survived infancy. Except for their deaths, her years in New Orleans were happy ones.

When the Civil War broke out, Sallie's activities became the subject of government reports — many thought she was a spy — but she proved to be a staunch Unionist. Leaving Hunt, a relative of Lexington guerilla leader Gen. John Hunt Morgan, in New Orleans, she returned to Louisville. Her husband gave his fortune to the Southern cause, and, at the end of the war, came to Louisville a poor man. They moved into a building on Jefferson Street, where he practiced medicine. When he died in 1867, he was buried from the Ward family mansion on Second Street. Sallie's father had passed away in 1862, before the war wiped out the family business. Widowed and no longer wealthy, Sallie lived for the next eight years upstairs over a barber shop at the Jefferson Street address, rearing her son. There were rumors she was writing her autobiography, but no manuscript was ever found.

On Monday, May 17, 1875, Col. M. Lewis Clark ran the first Kentucky Derby at his Louisville Jockey Club and Driving Park Association. Because of the free infield and pre-race publicity, the event drew a crowd of 10,000. Sallie Ward, famous Kentucky belle and beauty, *The Herald-Post* reported, occupied a box with a gay party. She may not have been rich, but she was still a lady to be reckoned with; her Johnson nephews were vice-presidents of the track! From the very beginning she gave Louisville racing her stamp of approval and put the Derby in a class by itself. When Churchill Downs published its first press book 60 years later, Sallie was still so well remembered that she and actress Mary Anderson were the only two attendees mentioned by name.

In 1875, Sallie's niece, Emily Ward, daughter of Matt and Anna Key, returned to Louisville to marry wealthy businessman and racing enthusiast, Henry Gilmore. By then, Sally had had enough of genteel poverty. The following June she married Vene P. Armstrong, a bluff, hearty pork-packer, long active in civic affairs. The Hardin County resident was a self-made man who got his start in business running the general store at West Point, Ky. As early as 1860, he had traveled all the way to Louisville for opening day at Woodlawn Race Course. A *Louisville Daily Journal* reporter wrote that Armstrong "brought sunshine into our sanctum yesterday with his joyous face and genial humor. He visits our city on business but will be visible to the naked eye this afternoon on the Woodlawn course where hundreds of friends will be pleased to grasp his manly hand again."

By the time Armstrong retired from business and married Sallie, he had represented Hardin County in the State Legislature and was very rich. Money, and his love of horse racing, no doubt made up for his lack of Bluegrass roots. He built her a house on the northwest corner of Third and Ormsby, but Sallie preferred the refined atmosphere of the new Galt House (the first one burned in 1865), built by her cousin, Gen. Jilson Payne Johnson, with its deep red plush Axminster carpeting and ceilings frescoed after "tasteful designs." From the Galt House, it was a straight shot out Fourth Street to the races, and Sallie's favorite shops were close at hand. At 50, Sallie was a handsome woman and a trendsetter. Louisville dressmakers worked overtime filling her orders, using the finest imported cloth for her costumes. Milliners stood at her beck and call. Many a fine-feathered bird ended up on Mrs. Armstrong's head. Whatever Sallie wore, women wanted. Done up in her favorite shade of lavender, she was no shy violet. New York writers called her one of the reigning queens of American society.

Vene Armstrong died a month before the 1877 Derby, leaving Sallie a considerable fortune. After observing a decent period of mourning, she appeared, dressed to the nines, at every gala affair in Louisville. Thanks to her, local day-after-Derby newspapers read like fashion magazines, with detailed accounts of who wore what, down to the smallest plume and button.

Sallie married a fourth and final time. In 1885 she became Mrs. G. F. Downs, wife of the man who had attended her fancy dress ball 35 years before. He was a wealthy widower whose children were far from pleased with the match. The newlyweds had a suite at the Galt House and in 1888, as Mrs. Downs, Sallie sold Armstrong's house at Third and Ormsby. Coincidentally, that same year, a Thoroughbred named Ward Gilmore in honor of Sallie's 8-year-old great-nephew, was entered in all the major stakes at the Churchill's racetrack, nicknamed "the downs" by 1883 — two years before the marriage that made Sallie a Downs as well.

Although in her 60s, Sallie remained, at least in her own mind, the belle of Louisville. She was rich. People catered to her. The only thing she couldn't command was time. She used makeup so heavily her face looked like a mask. The story is told that a laborer, seeing her as she emerged from a dress shop, exclaimed, "By God, she's painted!" Sallie coolly replied "Yes! Painted by God!" In her area of expertise, Sallie was never at a loss for words!

She went into seclusion in 1894, spending her days writing friends, designing her white satin shroud, overseeing work on her violet-colored casket, planning her funeral and giving her step-daughter advice on how to dress. Sallie died in July 1896 and was buried in the Ward lot at Cave Hill Cemetery — near her parents, Dr. Hunt and Vene Armstrong, her brother Matt and the infamous Anna Key, whose second daughter was named for Sallie.

On May 13, 1897, the day after the 23rd running of the Derby, *The Courier-Journal*'s society columnist noted that the most tasteful gown in the stand was worn by a Chicago woman, Mrs. Urquhart Lee, who sat in a box with Mrs. Emily Ward Gilmore and Mrs. Matt Ward. Mrs. Lee had on a stunning Napoleon blue and mandarin yellow original Paquin model from Paris and a very large Manila straw hat trimmed with white lace ruching, black ostrich tips and cornflowers. Only after death was Sallie Ward upstaged!

The last Sally Ward filly was registered with The Jockey Club in 1909. Sallie Ward Lawrence Hunt Armstrong Downs. She turned Louisville racing into a fashion statement. When Mrs. Downs was at the Downs, the Downs was the place to be.

**The New Louisville Jockey Club Grandstand
around the turn of the century.
Collection of The Filson Club Historical Society**

Chapter Six

Tough Times and Turf Exchanges

For some, wagering is racing's besetting sin. But pari-mutuel wagering is the payoff that puts feed in horses' mouths, supports the show and pays its way. Gambling fever, on the other hand, especially casino gambling fever, has run in 100-year cycles for the past 400 years, always cresting at the end of the century.

Critics called Charles II's reign one of the most corrupt in English history. His brother, James, enjoyed his sport and his mistresses almost as much Charles had and was deposed in 1688 only because he tried to return England to the Catholic Church. His successors, respectable Dutch co-monarchs William and Mary, seemed dull by comparison. But "serious and silent" William took racing to heart and was a heavy plunger, as bettors were called. Racetracks sprang up all over the country. In spite of an equine flu epidemic in 1699, there was more racing that year than ever before. By 1703, when Mary's sister, Anne, became queen, casino gambling had gotten totally out of hand. Church leaders petitioned Parliament to institute laws that limited betting to those who were sufficiently wealthy to cover their bets. Churches were not as concerned with the salvation of souls as with the burden of supporting families of men bankrupted and imprisoned as a result of wagering.

On the track, horse-owners, including Jockey Club gentlemen, were the biggest cheats. Ways to fix races were limited only by the owner's imagination and willingness to maim competitors' animals. Wealthy men attracted greedy, shiftless hangers-on. The Duke of Cumberland, head of the English Jockey Club, loved to gamble and settled his vast paunch under the card tables at Newmarket night after night, playing until dawn. He was an embarrassment the English Prime Minister referred to as the prodigal son of the fatted calf. Without regulation, racetracks became hangouts for pickpockets, prostitutes and card sharks. Roulette wheels were a feature at every course. In 1793, when English gambling got totally out of hand again, the tables at Doncaster were seized and burned in front of the clubhouse.

As gambling fever gripped America after the Revolutionary War, Northern states passed legislation that closed racetracks. Reforms came and went, depending on the state of the economy. Good times encouraged racing. Hard times snuffed it out. By 1850, English goings-on of the 1700s were mild in comparison to Victorian excesses. There were nearly 400 betting houses in London, of which perhaps 10 were solvent. They were a social evil, reformers preached, encouraging clerks to raid tills and servants to steal from their masters. "Honest racing" was a contradiction in terms. Horses were routinely sored, drugged, poisoned or filled with water and buckshot — hence the handicapping of races was impossible. Racing rules were an outmoded muddle, allowing owners to pay small fines for cheating on course. The self-serving Jockey Club was in a state of near moral and financial collapse.

The turf needed more than reform, it needed commitment, clout and vigilance to restore its fading luster. Reform emerged in the person of Adm. Henry John Rous, younger son of the Earl of Stradbroke, whose family stables were at Suffolk. By the time Rous' naval career ended in 1829, he had been a member of the Jockey Club for eight years. He married wealth and represented Westminster in Parliament from 1841 to 1846, but nothing delighted him like racing. He proceeded to devote his life to the sport, becoming permanent president of the Jockey Club.

First he straightened out its finances, then he tackled the rule book. In 1850 he published *The Laws and Practice of Horse Racing*, which contained a history of the Thoroughbred; explained stewards' and racing officials' duties; listed rules and cited examples of how these rules were to be applied to the sport. Rous vehemently opposed heavy betting because so many of his own class had been ruined by it. He respected honest bookmakers, knowing that the sport needed wagering to survive. Once his position as public handicapper was secure, the energetic Rous watched racing from every point on the track. From turrets atop stands he surveyed the field through his naval telescope. If he heard rumors of a jockey not trying to win, he hid himself in the shrubbery, leaped out and roared at the offender as he went by. Rous believed firmly that jockeys needed to be kept in their place. He used the terms "training groom" and "riding groom" instead of trainer and jockey, to show these men how humble their place should be. Rous' rulings weren't always evenhanded, but he brought stability to the sport, becoming English racing's "dictator" long before his death in 1877. He had considerable impact on American racing; he was M. Lewis Clark's mentor the year Clark studied

English racing.

Once racing results could be telegraphed, bookmaking operations called turf exchanges sprang up around America. Bookmakers claimed they were the same as the Wall Street Stock Exchange — once the Wall and Water Street hangout of slave-traders, money-changers and the notorious pirate, "Blue Beard." Except for the fact that it was faster to lose money betting on a horse than on grain futures or the price of gold, certain undeniable similarities did exist.

Saratoga Spa, in upstate New York, led the way as a gaming center frequented by the nouveau riche. Racing horses was a way to gain social acceptability or land a titled Englishman for one's daughter. The goings-on at Saratoga were such that *Godey's Lady's Book* called it the Sodom and Gomorrah of the Union. There, "women painted their eyes, wore false busts and false hair in bags behind their heads." To what extremes, *Godey's* editorialized, may we not expect the dear creatures to go?

Saratoga was the resort of dandies, thugs and politicians; "Diamond Jim" Brady, John W. "Bet-a-Million" Gates (his fortune came from selling barbed wire to western ranchers), the lecherous old Dutch buccaneer Cornelius Van Derbilt — a trotting horse man; and a gambling house operator from Versailles, Ky., named Henry Price McGrath. These were ruthless, self-made men who appeared in New York from the Western gold fields and Pennsylvania coal mines. Wherever they found opportunities to ravage the environment and destroy their fellow men they were eager for the task — a philosophy best expressed in William Vanderbilt's immortal words — "The public be damned."

There was Andrew Carnegie and his bookkeeper, the cobbler's son, Henry Phipps, who ran their steel mills on other people's money. "What we used to admire about Phipps," a Pittsburgh banker said, "was the way he could keep a check dangling in the air for two or three days."

From San Francisco came Darius Ogden Mills, a former storekeeper, who arrived in New York one day with his gold from the Sierras and purchased, at the highest price ever paid for city real estate, a lot on Fifth Avenue opposite St. Patrick's Cathedral. Mills gave carte blanche to New York decorators, left for California and returned to a house fit for an Oriental potentate. The $450,000 bill disturbed him. Mills had no idea that culture would cost so much!

Railroad baron Jay Gould, the "Mephistopheles of Wall Street," whose stock manipulations touched off the 1873 Panic, was considered too vulgar even for this bunch, so his son became the first Gould admitted to "polite" society. Phipps, Mills and Gould, along with Frick, Fisk, Morgan, Payne and Philadelphia butcher Peter A. B. Widener, were all robber barons, but measured in terms of sheer wealth and meanness they couldn't touch John Jacob Astor, a German immigrant to the colonies before the Revolution. Astor apprenticed himself to a furrier, then headed west to barter for pelts with the Native American tribes. By 1820, Astor's American Fur Company stretched from Missouri to Canada. His agents traded furs for whiskey, and, according to Congressional reports, it was tainted whiskey at that! Astor bought real estate — miles of New York tenements. Under the watchful eye of John Jacob's second son, William Backhouse Astor, the Astor fortune grew by leaps and bounds. When William died, his sons, William, Jr. and John Jacob III, each inherited over $20 million, tax-free.

The Astors and their ilk were very rich; they just weren't respectable. So they built mansions, bought art by the trainload, endowed universities and hired genealogists who "found" ancestors for them among ancient Scottish kings and German nobility. Suitably pedigreed, they arranged for their children to marry into good old families — disastrous unions that not infrequently led to divorce and suicide — so they could become part of the social order Mrs. William B. Astor, Jr. called her "Four Hundred." Lastly, they bought Thoroughbreds, registered their silks in sporting newspapers they controlled, and went to Saratoga. When travel to Saratoga became inconvenient, the Four Hundred brought racing back to the city.

Leonard Jerome was a Wall Street multi-millionaire who developed a fetish for exclusive sports. He loved his horses far more than he loved his wife. While living abroad, she engineered their daughter's marriage to Lord Randolph Churchill, younger son of the Duke of Marlborough. That unhappy alliance produced Winston Leonard Spencer Churchill, the great English Prime Minister — but no relation to the Churchill family of Louisville racetrack fame.

With help from German-born financier August Belmont and playboy William Travers, Jerome organized the American Jockey Club and built a magnificent track in New York's suburbs. Jerome Park's opening meet in 1866 attracted such connoisseurs of Thoroughbred pedigree as former circus barker and railroad manipulator,

Col. James Fisk, Jr.; Tammany Hall's "Boss" Tweed; soon to be scandal-ridden President Gen. Ulysses S. Grant; and Josie Woods, proprietor of the fanciest whorehouse in the city.

The 1873 Panic ruined Jerome, but immigrants kept right on living in Astors' tenements. William Backhouse Astor designated his oldest son, John Jacob III, overseer of the family's fortune. That left his surly younger son, William B., Jr. (sometimes referred to as "Outhouse" Astor) with nothing to do except spend money. Young William married into an old New York Dutch family whose enterprising founder made his fortune selling guns to the Indians. Caroline Schermerhorn made herself queen of American society with Astor money. William, not cut out to be her "king," bought a yacht, retreated to his country estate, and raced horses on the Eastern circuit. Occasionally, he disappeared into the wilds of Minnesota on drinking binges; then he headed for Jacksonville, Fla., where he founded the Florida Yacht Club and became notorious for his "orgies at sea." He buried his father late in 1875, married off his daughter on March 1, 1876, and left for Florida the next day.

Astor was next heard from in *Turf, Field and Farm* as the owner of Vagrant, five days after the Kentucky Derby was run. For the Derby, Vagrant ran in Astor's silks but the gelding's former owner, T. J. Nichols of Paris, Ky., collected the winner's purse. The Kentucky-based *Thoroughbred Record*, published by Benjamin Gratz Bruce, never acknowledged the sale and always referred to Vagrant as Nichols' Derby winner. Whatever the story behind the 1876 Derby, there was no love lost between Bruce and William B. Astor, Jr.

By the 1880s, New York society included Vanderbilts, Whitneys, Phipps, the second generation Goulds, Rockefellers, and Huntingtons. They threw lavish parties. They built the Metropolitan Opera so they could sit in the best boxes. Aping English aristocracy, they created exclusive sporting clubs for yachting, tennis and racing, so as to appear "to the manner born."

Such was their vanity and utterly lacking sense of noblesse oblige that when Clark called for a meeting in Louisville to discuss problems common to all tracks, the American Jockey Club ignored the invitation, the only one of the 11 nationwide racing organizations not to attend. A report of the conference called it "harmonious, one of the most important events in the history of the American turf. . . its influence for good to be felt throughout the country." *The Thoroughbred Record*'s editor only hoped New York's absent plutocrats would endorse the reforms.

As the "Sport of Kings" turned rotten to the core — driven by the very excesses New York fortunes were built on — the American Jockey Club evolved into The Jockey Club, dedicated to imposing its sense of order on Thoroughbred racing. Formed in 1894, it was too elite and too out of touch to save even New York racing.

Throughout the 20 years Clark ruled the Downs, his philosophy about gambling was based on Rous' rules. Clark imported French pari-mutuel machines ("pari" is French for bet; "mutuel" means a benefit association established for the common good) and had them on track by Derby Day in 1875. There was some question as to their legality — machine gambling had long been outlawed in the state — so they did not reappear until 1878, after the Kentucky Legislature approved their use. Through 1881, pari-mutuel machines and auction pools were the only two ways to wager. Then Clark bowed to public pressure and struck a deal with bookmakers in 1882 as a means of attracting both entrants and patrons. So important was wagering that when torrential rains threatened Derby attendance on May 22, 1883, Clark rescheduled the race for the following day. On the eve of the 1886 Derby, Clark and the bookmakers had a falling out over contract terms. Clark banned them from the track before the race, thereby alienating big New York stables whose owners were heavy bettors. When Yankee horse-owners threatened to boycott Louisville racing altogether the following spring, Clark had no choice but to let out-of-town bookmakers return for the 1887 Derby.

One of the little-noticed local reactions to this was the announcement that 13 local businessmen were forming a new Jockey Club with plans to lease the old Greeneland track. Incorporators included bookmaker Emile Boulier and A. Harthill, a horse doctor recently come to town from Canada. For reasons unknown, nothing came of their plans.

In 1889, *The Critic* noted: "Poolrooms are getting as thick as poker rooms. Is it necessary to the well being and prosperity of citizens that poolrooms should be open the year around?" From 1890 until 1908, neither auction pools (in which wagerers "bought" the horse they backed for the duration of the race) nor pari-mutuels were permitted at the Downs.

Once big-time gamblers got a stranglehold on racing, things went from bad to worse. The increasingly intemperate Clark couldn't stem the tide in Louisville as end-of-century gambling fever spread like wildfire and engulfed urban tracks. Within months of the formation of the exclusive New York Jockey Club, *THE LOUISVILLE COMMERCIAL* carried the details of the Louisville Jockey Club's insolvency.

On August 7, 1894, Clark paid all the Club's bills and turned the operation over to a group of local bookmakers, headed by William F. Schulte, incorporated as the New Louisville Jockey Club. Within the month, the new owners began widening and regrading the track with an eye toward renting it to the newly formed Louisville Fair and Driving Association, which scheduled a meet there in October 1894. From time to time Clark had scheduled hurdle races at the Downs — *THE LOUISVILLE COMMERCIAL* even mentioned jackrabbit racing in the infield on the 1889 Fourth of July program — but Standardbred racing had heretofore been confined to nearby Douglas Park. The same fall that trotters raced at the Downs, a comely Japanese housewife went cycling in Cherokee Park wearing bloomers. Louisvillians shook their heads and wondered what the world was coming to! Mayor Tyler proclaimed Oct. 24, 1894, a half-holiday, so city employees could attend the Meet. The three-day effort was a disaster and there were no more Fall Meets of any kind at "Church Hill Downs" from 1896 through 1904.

During that decade, there was a marked change in the way Thoroughbreds were handled. The public trainer came into his own. Without state racing commissions to license or monitor horse ownership, turf exchange owners bought the horses on which they made book. W. E. Applegate, Emil Bourlier and Henry Wehmhoff were well-known local horse-owning bookmakers — and very prosperous men. When Bourlier's widow married a man half her age in 1902, the newspaper noted that she had inherited a substantial fortune. Like the bartenders of old, local bookmakers tended to monitor those who frequented their establishments, and were known to turn away individuals who habitually "invested" more on local races than their families could afford, but interstate wagering, made possible by the Western Union telegraph system, was impossible to control, although Missouri tried. Late in 1894, it became the first state to pass a law prohibiting the sale of pools on races run outside the state. Betting was limited to pools sold at the track.

To the outrage of decent citizens, the road to the Downs became a "no-man's-land" filled with lowlife who disappeared into the woods the few times police showed up to arrest them. Reporters wrote about the beautifully-dressed prostitutes who sat in carriages right outside the track entrance on P Street (Central Avenue). A uniformed Black footman carried their wagers to and from the betting shed. Prostitution was frowned on, but not suppressed. Up until World War I, "sporting houses" ranged the length of Green Street, renamed Liberty Street after these brothels were closed. In tasteful brochures distributed to conventioneers, madams bragged about their girls and the fine cuisine available in their establishments. It was all part of the ambiance that made Louisville the Gateway to the South!

After the Derby distance was shortened by a quarter-mile in 1896, nominations tripled, but very few horses showed up for the race. From 1895 to 1904, there were only 53 Derby contestants, an average of less than six per year. Spring Meets went steadily downhill until, after the 1902 Derby, even the bookmakers threw in the towel. Newspapers described the Derby that year as "not much of a contest." After the Oaks, the headlines read: "Racing Over — Everyone Glad." Nine days, the article concluded, was more racing than Louisville would stand for.

Because of Louisville's powerful Protestant church coalition, the anti-gambling movement gained momentum here earlier than it did in New York. Its resolution here was also relatively peaceful because of the highly effective way Matt Winn reorganized the Downs after the disastrous 1902 Spring Meet. But even under Winn's leadership, the track struggled for respectability. At the 1906 Fall Meet, two bookmakers exchanged blows in the betting shed amid rumors of race fixing. The offender, who shot his opponent's cashier, was promptly taken before a local magistrate, who "happened to be on the grounds" and the bookie's $500 bond was quickly guaranteed by friends. Such had become the Sport of Kings.

The 1897 Depression had taken a tremendous toll of New York Thoroughbred racing as stable after stable went bankrupt. Lexington breeders retrenched accordingly. Horses not sold for slaughter ended up as polo ponies in South America or turned out on the Texas range to refine Quarter Horse stock. When James Ben Ali Haggin sold over 100 yearlings at England's Tattersalls auction in 1899, the Weatherbys, official Keepers of British Thoroughbred records, were not pleased to enter the pedigrees of these cheaply-bought "colonial halfbreeds" in their *General Stud Book*. Ten years later, when 100 more American Thoroughbreds were auctioned at Newmarket, the Weatherbys dug in their heels. They didn't remove the names of Haggin's Thoroughbreds, but they refused to add the new batch to the record books. American owners in the throes of their own racing battles paid scant attention to the news.

Jockey Club members who survived the 1897 recession were too wealthy to be unhorsed — or so they thought. Just as smaller stables began to rebound from the recession, New York faced bigger challenges. The excesses associated with track and off-site gambling operations brought about agitation for sorely-needed reform. From 1895 to 1908, New York racing operated under the Percy-Gray Law making poolrooms and bookmaking illegal, but allowing individuals on racetracks to wager among themselves. New York racing was at its height when reports of corruption, written by legislative counsel Charles Evans Hughes, later two-term governor of New York and Chief Justice of the United States Supreme Court, brought out anti-gambling advocates by the droves, somewhat dampening fans' interest in the sport. Belmont Park increased the admission fee to $3 to offset the attendance decline. When that cut admissions even more, August Belmont recommended the fee be raised to $5, "to keep away from Jockey Club supervised courses such persons as are unable to patronize so costly a sport."

In June 1908, anti-gambling legislation closed New York tracks. Southern breeders, who suffered most from a shutdown of their biggest market, panicked. A month later, a Charlottesville, Va., horseman sent a letter to the *Thoroughbred Record. "Like Foxhall Daingerfield,"* he wrote, *"I am not thunderstruck over Hughes' bill, but rather think it will prove a blessing to the small but refined breeder. The business was greatly overdone. We did not ship yearlings to New York this year. My son Arthur went there to see what the Jockey Club will do. Meanwhile we will cut our broodmares down to thirty or less and raise more cattle and sheep. Pray pardon the liberty I take to write you. It is the view of one who has been raising thoroughbred racehorses and shorthorn cattle for thirty-six years."* The letter was signed "R. J. Hancock."

Shortly thereafter, young Arthur Hancock moved to Kentucky and established Claiborne Farm on Bourbon County land where a Virginia farmer, Alexander Breckenridge, first bred and raced Thoroughbreds in the 1830s. Hancock and his descendants have since had an enormous influence on the Thoroughbred industry nationwide.

Matt Winn reintroduced pari-mutuel wagering at the 1908

Derby and at nearby Douglas Park which, by then, he also headed. Pari-mutuel wagering proved so unpopular at chronically ill-fated Douglas Park that Winn gave up and turned the track over to Louis Cella, a St. Louis bookmaker.

That same year, the New York Court of Appeals decided oral betting between individuals did not constitute bookmaking. New York tracks cautiously reopened in 1909, with only admission fees to pay their expenses, nonetheless determined to stay afloat.

By 1910, there were five pari-mutuel machines in place for Lexington's Kentucky Association Spring Meet and $2 and $5 ticket sales were brisk. Eugene Elrod, the Downs' betting ring supervisor, went to Lexington to set the machines up. For the 1910 Derby, the infield was free and pari-mutuel business much improved. On April 25, 1910, two weeks before Derby Day in Louisville, New York's Governor Hughes accepted appointment to the United States Supreme Court. On May 26, the Agnew-Perkins Bill, making directors of racing associations criminally liable for any betting, oral, written or by machine, taking place on their tracks, became law in New York. At its annual mid-August Saratoga board meeting, The Jockey Club agreed to shut down New York racing after Aug. 31, 1910. Members concluded that "racing would not be profitable under the prevailing conditions." In September, they began shipping their Thoroughbreds to South America, France and England.

Argentina responded within the month, barring horses not bred in Argentina from virtually all competition. England followed suit in a more democratic fashion. An early December *Thoroughbred Record* reported that "a petition to the [English] Jockey Club stewards has been prepared, the object being to restrict the importation (for sale) of American yearlings and older racing stock." In 1913, Lord Jersey chaired an English Jockey Club committee which directed Weatherbys to list only such Thoroughbreds in its *General Stud Book* as could "trace without flaw on both sire's and dam's side to horses and mares themselves already accepted in the earlier volumes of this book." The "Jersey Act" was not amended until 1949, when American Thoroughbreds looked pretty good to war-ravaged England.

By late 1911 it was more profitable to ship mares — numbers of which died en route from trauma — to Australia than to auction them in Lexington, Ky. Faced with registering ever-diminishing numbers of Thoroughbreds, Algernon Daingerfield, The

Jockey Club's assistant secretary, surveyed the crisis and wrote: "It's not the money or the sentiment, it's about the danger to the future of the character of the American horse." The Jockey Club that had once registered 4,700 foals was registering less than a thousand. That number was expected to drop in 1912. The list of those racing abroad read like a New York society *Who's Who*. Harry Payne Whitney nominated more than 20 horses for the English Oaks and Derby. William Astor Chandler, Ogden Bishop, James B. Haggin, James R. Keene, Frank Gould, Alex Cochrane, DeCourcey Forbes, and Perry Belmont were all in France, where Jockey Club chairman August Belmont had shipped his racing stables and established a breeding farm. When France excluded imported Thoroughbreds from flat races, the horses became steeplechasers. Russia and Austria were added to the list of countries gobbling up American Thoroughbreds and American jockeys to boot.

In its darkest hour, American racing was virtually abandoned by those most able to afford the struggle to keep it on track. The sport and the industry needed a leader the likes of which it had never had before. The rest of the story — of the Louisville-born immigrant Irish grocer's son who saved American racing — was about to unfold.

Colonel Matt J. Winn

Chapter Seven

Betting on Winn

"He has seen them all!" reads the legend under Matt Winn's picture on Churchill Downs' 1949 Diamond Jubilee Derby glass. But Winn had done more than just see every Derby since 1875. Late in 1902 he led a group of seven local businessmen in a rescue operation to save the Downs. Indeed, without Winn's stylish leadership, the Derby would have been dead by 1903, done in by bookmakers and Clark's clannish elitism.

That it is the only race in America run at the same site every spring for 121 years, and that, as the sun sets on the first Saturday in May, the eyes of the world are on Louisville, is Matt Winn's doing. He was there at the birth of the Downs, then called the Louisville Jockey Club and Driving Park Association, a 13-year-old standing on the seat of his father's produce wagon in the free-gate zone, today's legendary infield. Winn's father was an Irish immigrant whose grocery store was in Portland, west of Louisville, on the Ohio River. Winn's father wasn't a horse player, but opening day at the Louisville Jockey Club wasn't horse racing; it was an extravaganza that had been three years in the planning.

The Winns went the track in time to see the parade of carriages filled with ladies dressed in Paris gowns, accompanied by the city's wealthiest men; they were all part of the show. A select few, Louisville Jockey Club members — wearing miniature silver horseshoe badges in their lapels — shared the exclusive clubhouse with their guests. It was a day Winn loved to talk about — how the favorite, Chesapeake, started his big stretch run, then fell back exhausted as his stablemate, Aristides, surged to the lead like a whirlwind, setting a new world's record for a mile and a half race.

In 1884, *THE LOUISVILLE COMMERCIAL* previewed the Derby as "A Great Gathering of Cracks at Churchill Downs," headlining the name by which the Louisville Jockey Club's track would eventually be known. Winn went back every spring because the infield was free. In 1886 he arrived too late to buy into the auction pools, so he made his way to the "French pools," imported parimutuel machines, and bought $5 place tickets on Blue Wing, then climbed onto the shed roof not far from the finish line. The race developed into a furious stretch battle between Blue Wing and James Ben Ali Haggin's Ben Ali. In the excitement, the rooftoppers fell, knocking Winn off his perch. "Even as I was falling," he remembered, "I found a little opening between bodies, saw the horses for a fleeting fraction of a second as they roared across the finish line, and it looked as if it was Ben Ali by a nose — which, officially, it was." Untangling himself from the heap, Winn collected his winnings and went home a happy man.

Haggin, a big bettor, was enraged because Colonel Clark barred bookmakers from the Derby that year after a contract dispute. Well before dawn, Haggin's entire stable was on its way back to New York. Such was his clout that it would be 25 years before Eastern owners, wooed by the man who saw his first Derby from the infield, sent horses to Louisville again.

There was so much racing by the end of the 1880s that Clark was forced to let bookmakers back in, but Louisville drew fewer and fewer good horses. Derby attendance declined; even a full house on Derby Day didn't attract repeat customers, in spite of what businessmen and stockholders did to promote the Downs. "Two Street Railways have been finished out to the course," the 1890 Spring Meet program noted. "The Horse cars leave the Galt House, Louisville Hotel and also the corner of Fourth and Main every two minutes, carrying passengers to within 50 feet of the stand." Third Street had been finished with asphalt pavement as far as the House of Refuge, then connected with a well-sprinkled dirt road to the grounds, making it "one of the loveliest drives in the country." The program didn't mention the bands of petty thieves, pickpockets and prostitutes who lined the route.

In 1894, the New Louisville Jockey Club — a group of local bookmakers — bought the Downs and invested $100,000 to upgrade the site. They closed Clark's leaky clubhouse and built a twin-steepled grandstand, attached to a huge betting shed, office and saddling paddock, on the northwest side of the track. Two years later a band shell was added in the infield, providing Derby-goers with such lively syncopations as "My Gal's a High-Born Lady" and "In Gay New York."

Many of the horses that ran at the Downs from 1895 to 1902 were either bookmaker's horses or from stables bookmakers controlled. National turf writers weren't interested in Louisville racing — or band music — especially when there was reason to believe that winners were decided long before the horses ever set foot on the track. Race-fixing was by no means limited to Louisville. Conditions in New York were so bad a group of multi-millionaires — men to whom racing was only an expensive hobby — formed their own Jockey Club to preserve what they termed "honest sport."

Winn, meanwhile, was becoming a turn-of-the-century success story. After completing business school, he worked for a grocery company, traveling around Kentucky wholesaling staples and buying produce for the Louisville store. In 1887, his tailor offered the tall, blue-eyed, soft-spoken Irishman a partnership. As the firm's salesman and personal representative, Winn traveled the circuit to New Orleans, southwest through El Paso, all the way to Los Angeles. Wherever there were men with money, he was there to measure them for custom made suits. E. R. Bradley, an El Paso gambler, was one of Winn's first clients. The men developed a lifelong friendship that stood Winn in good stead when Bradley's Idle Hour Farm Thoroughbreds raced at the Downs.

Winn attended the Derby every year, proving himself a topnotch handicapper. At the close of the 1902 Spring Meet, newsman Charlie Price, secretary of the New Louisville Jockey Club, offered Winn the operation for $40,000, not including the land, which Churchill heirs still owned. Without a buyer, Churchill Downs was about to become the fourth unsuccessful racetrack in Louisville's history, a remarkably bad record for a city situated 75 miles from the heart of Thoroughbred country. Winn was the last hope. Everybody else had laughed at Price's proposition because all but diehard gamblers considered the Downs more of a liability than an asset. Without an immediate buyer, the Derby was dead.

At 41, married, the father of eight daughters, Winn was in no position to take risks. He called friends, and business associates like hotelman Louis Seelbach, brewer Frank Fehr and manufacturer Charles F. Grainger. All were self-made men without family fortunes to back them. Together, they came up with $40,000, chose Grainger as president, and began planning for the 1903 Derby. They sold 200 memberships at $100 each by promising buyers exclusive seating. With that $20,000, Winn built a clubhouse on the finish line, next to the grandstand. His aim was to turn the track into a place where people felt welcome. The clubhouse and grandstand were full the following spring and the track showed a profit for the first time in its history. Winn's partners asked him to manage the operation. With a family to support, he turned them down. The investors stood firm. Winn consulted his wife whom he loved dearly. She had been at his side since 1889 when Spokane beat Proctor Knott and he collected $34.80 for every $2 pari-mutuel ticket he bought. She gave him $10 that day — all the money she had. Now she encouraged him to risk everything again. Late in 1903, Winn sold his interest in the tailoring business and became the track's vice-president and general manager. "I immediately ceased being a horse player," he wrote in his memoirs. "I never bet as much as a cigar on the outcome of any race since that time."

Those years as a salesman stood him in good stead. There was no Sallie Ward or Madame Modjeska for the crowds to glimpse, but ever so often, while he was rebuilding the track's reputation, he snagged a star like actress Lillian Russell, who attended the Derby in 1905, the same year the Churchill Downs site was finally purchased from the Churchill heirs.

Winn hired entertainment, paying $5,000 for John Philip Sousa's band to perform at the Downs. It was all part of a strategy that set the Downs apart from the usual approach to racetrack utilization. Winn had not become a winning handicapper by sitting in the clubhouse. He was an infield and backside man. He knew Kentucky, and Kentucky politics, like the back of his hand. He had traveled nationwide when that meant unheated trains, eating at dirty diners, and a lot of walking. He had done it all and he was about to do it again.

In 1904, rival Western Turf Association tracks, headed by St. Louis bookmaker Louis Cella, ignored Winn's request for more and better racing dates. Winn pulled out of the Association, taking nine other disgruntled track owners with him. They formed the American Turf Association, with Winn as president. Stable by stable, horsemen and jockeys defected to Winn's group during a two-year struggle that ended in the creation of a Kentucky State Racing Commission empowered to license tracks and award racing dates. By then, Winn was also managing Louisville's Douglas Park track. Over the next two years, Winn fought three major "turf wars," each time outmaneuvering major opposition, including the powerful New York Jockey Club, whose members he converted into some of his staunchest allies. Winn traveled everywhere. As president of the American Turf Association, he managed racetracks from New Orleans to Yonkers. All this was merely practice for the battle ahead.

By the turn of the century, as people saw unregulated racing become a public nuisance that attracted the dregs of society to their communities, anti-gambling groups sprung up nationwide. Churches bore the brunt of supporting families where gambling was a parental addiction. Businessmen, whose employees stole from them to pay bookmakers, questioned the economic benefits of what had long since ceased to be a sport.

Local reformers targeted the Downs and Charlie Grainger, then Mayor of Louisville as well as track president, as the most visible symbols of corruption outside the Buckingham Theatre, where "Boss" Whallen presided over the city's convention-related vices, ably assisted by Harry Brennan, millionaire son of Irish immigrant Brennan Plow Company founder, Thomas Brennan. To make matters worse, Grainger had appointed Winn Director of Safety. In that capacity, Winn supervised the largely Irish police and fire departments, issued licenses for sporting events and kept reform-minded churchmen cooling their heels in his office for days at a time. When the reformers ended up winning the much-disputed 1905 election in a 1907 State Court decision, Governor Cripps Beckham appointed County Attorney and reform movement leader, Robert Worth Bingham, to serve as Mayor and Winn was ousted from his political job.

Louisville promptly passed ordinances barring bookmakers from plying their trade within the city limits, leaving only the high-priced auction pools for the wagering public to use. Winn cancelled plans for the Fall Meet after Sheriff Alexander Scott Bullitt announced he would raid the betting ring each day and arrest everyone attempting to make a book. The following February, newly-elected Sheriff Charles Scholl announced his intentions to carry out Sheriff Bullitt's directives at the Spring Meet as well.

Winn responded by stating that only pari-mutuel wagering would be permitted at the 1908 Derby. City officials quickly pointed out that gambling machines violated a 19th Century Kentucky law aimed at outlawing roulette wheels, but Winn remembered cashing pari-mutuel tickets in the 1880s. He knew Colonel Clark had imported pari-mutuel machines before the first Derby, but hadn't actually used them until 1878. Something accounted for that three year delay and Winn set himself to the task of discovering what it was. He found the answer in an 1878 amendment to the Kentucky Statutes prohibiting machine wagering. The words that saved the Derby were: "This act shall not apply to persons who may sell combination, or French pools, on any regular race track during the races thereon." Louisville business interests lobbied hard to slip that exemption through the Legislature. Besides the Downs and the Derby, it is probably the Churchill family's greatest contribution to American racing.

Winn ordered 15 new pari-mutuel machines. In his autobiography he tells a fanciful story about retrieving the old machines from basements, storerooms, a pawn shop and New York tracks, where they had been used briefly in the 1870s, but the March 28, 1908 *Thoroughbred Record* stated that 11 machines, the likes of which had not been seen for 30 years, had been delivered to the Downs. When Winn ran full-page newspaper ads explaining the mathematics of pari-mutuel wagering, City Hall threatened to arrest anyone caught placing a bet at the track, but, at the last minute, a Circuit Court judge granted an injunction against such governmental highhandedness. The headlines brought crowds to the Downs for the Derby. If nothing else, they were there to watch a good fight. What Derby-goers saw in the betting shed were pari-mutuel machines, each equipped with a telephone and staffed with a clerk selling pari-mutuel tickets — little multi-colored chits — bearing Winn's signature. When the windows closed before each race, ticket sellers phoned in the number of wagers made. Men in the cashier's room figured the payoffs while the horses were on the track.

Fans were more excited about the 1908 Derby than most horse owners were. Of the 13 horses supposed to run, only eight went to the gate. Except for Louisvillian George R. Long's Bashford Manor Stables, no other owners had ever entered a Derby before. Slowgoing Stone Street, whose sole career victory was the Derby, won the race by three lengths, paying $123.50 for a $5 bet. The payoff made the meaning of the term "wagering among ourselves" perfectly clear. The following day the Kentucky Court of Appeals held that pari-mutuel wagering was legal on a racetrack during a meet. "The future of Thoroughbred racing, which had hung in the balance for months, was settled and would continue undisturbed," *The Thoroughbred Record* concluded.

Anti-gambling forces already had such a stranglehold on the New York Legislature, eastern Thoroughbred owners held their breath that Derby Day. The following Monday, Winn wrote Algernon Daingerfield at The Jockey Club in New York City: "My Dear Sir: Hooray. Very Truly, M.J. Winn." Winn's usually small, meticulous handwriting sprawled triumphantly across the whole page. For Winn's service to the Commonwealth, Gov. Cripps Beckham appointed him to the state's honorary militia. Winn was now a real Kentucky Colonel.

As anti-gambling sentiment swept the country, the ban on bookmaking spread but pari-mutuel wagering grew. Winn hired a draftsman named Schuman to improve the machines, which Churchill Downs' president Charlie Grainger manufactured at his foundry and distributed throughout the country. In 1911, the cost of a bet was lowered from $5 to $2, enticing even timid bettors to try their luck.

By then, reformers had shut down New York racing and brought the industry to its knees in the East and South. With nowhere to run their horses, Kentucky Thoroughbred farms faced ruin. Winn tried to keep the southern half of the circuit open by building a racetrack in Mexico City. After the first meet he locked the door and threw the key away. It was useless to try to compete with the bull ring down the street. The track he managed in Juarez from 1909 to 1917 was a different story altogether. Racing was profitable but the politics were deadly. Pancho Villa was only one of the fully armed and trigger-happy visitors with whom Winn dealt. The two men hit it off so well, Winn told the story of complaining to Villa about the amount of hay locals were stealing from racetrack barns. The next day Juarez was plastered with notices: ANYONE WHO MOLESTS EL COLONEL WINN, OR ANY OF THE PROPERTY OF THE JUAREZ RACE TRACK, WILL BE SHOT. VILLA. If the Colonelcy had not been bestowed on Winn by frequent Derby visitor Governor Beckham before Winn went to Mexico, he certainly earned it under fire while he was there!

The man who put himself in charge of feeding Juarez racing patrons was Harry M. Stevens, who had already made a fortune feeding baseball fans his portable, spiced sandwich — the hot dog. Stevens loved racing, and from time to time accepted Thoroughbreds in exchange for unpaid food bills run up by down-on-their-luck trainers. He and Winn became good friends and Stevens kept the food service contract with Churchill Downs all his life.

During the decade of reform, Winn continued to monitor company interests at tracks in New York, Maryland and Illinois. He worked to change the public's concept of what a racetrack was, becoming to racing what showman P. T. Barnum had been to the circus. Under Winn's direction, the southend Downs became a rallying point for the whole community. In 1910, Glenn Curtiss, founder of Curtiss-Wright Aviation, shipped two unassembled airplanes by rail to the Downs, reassembled them and flew around the infield at a special two-day meet — the first recorded flight in the state. Between 60 m.p.h. dashes in front of the grandstand, 175 feet above the ground, that threw smoke in the spectator's faces, there were motorcycle races for the 10,000 Louisvillians who braved rain and 90 degree heat to find out what aviation was all about.

After the 1911 Derby, *The Thoroughbred Record* reported that moving picture men got footage of every incident preceding the running of the big event, and the race itself, from barrier rise to finish. "The pictures will be exhibited all over the country as soon as they are developed," the article concluded.

When the weather didn't cooperate on Derby Day, Winn's track superintendent, English landscape architect Tom Young, worked magic. Derby Day 1914 dawned clear, but nearly a week of bad weather had left the track muddy. Young and his crew went out at dawn with buckets and literally sponged the track dry enough, so the story goes, for a gelding named Old Rosebud to set a track record. Old Rosebud's owner was H. C. "Ham" Applegate, the Downs' auditor, and son of one of the local bookmakers who had bought the track in 1895. "Old Buddy"'s win was no fluke, however. He was recognized as the best horse in America in 1917 when he won 15 of 21 starts. He was destroyed at Jamaica racetrack in New York in 1922 after stepping in a hole and tearing ligaments in his ankle. The injury wasn't life-threatening, but the gelding would have been lame for the rest of his life and was of no use in the breeding shed, Applegate explained.

In 1915, the first four-legged "belle," Regret, won the Derby, running as favorite in the largest-ever Derby field. Winn had bent over backwards to get H. P. Whitney's stakes-winning 2-year-old filly's name in the entry box, even sending a letter to Daingerfield in February, 1915. By then, the Irish grocer's son addressed the Secretary of the Jockey Club on a first name basis: "Dear Algie, Have written to Jimmy Rowe [Regret's trainer] and to Sam Hildreth with regard to entries for the Kentucky Derby and, if you can bring the matter to their attention, wish you would ask them to make entries of their good ones, even if they are only complimentary, as the names of Regret and such horses would do us a lot of good in an advertising way." Two years before, Roscoe Goose had ridden longshot Donerail to a victory that paid $184.90 for a $2 bet. What better advertising could Winn want?

By 1916 Winn wrote to Daingerfield about a 20% business increase at the just concluded Spring Meet. He enclosed a day-after-Derby editorial from *The Courier-Journal* which read in part, "Such a day's sport as that of yesterday for those who went to see the Derby and such a day's business for the turf, cannot be looked upon by reasonable persons as a blot upon the escutcheon of the city or the State. It cannot cause regret that Kentucky was not swept by the anti-racing wave, partly made up of righteous puritanism, but partly of narrow and ignorant fanaticism, which destroyed the turf in a number of states less interested in breeding."

As revenue-producing pari-mutuel wagering supplanted unlicensed bookmaking, the wrath of reformers abated. By the late teens, American tracks were paying state taxes, Federal taxes and excess profits taxes. Racing enriched the nation in more ways than one. By 1918, *The Courier-Journal*'s owner, Robert Worth Bingham, who had led the reform movement to curb vice and close the track in 1905, was serving on the Downs' board.

When America went to war in 1917, Winn pledged 10% of all money the track handled to the Red Cross; employees gave 10% of their salaries; the track, 10% of its "take;" and the horsemen, 10% of their earnings. Betting became positively patriotic! During a nationwide potato shortage in 1918, Winn turned the Downs infield into a huge potato patch. When the crop was sold, all the profits went to the Red Cross. It was money sorely needed as soldiers returning from Europe brought with them a lethal influenza, the likes of which America had never experienced before.

Months after Exterminator won the 1918 Derby, Winn announced that geldings would not be allowed to compete in the 1919 Derby. The government needed Thoroughbreds for breeding purposes and the only way to meet that need, Winn reasoned, was to make it unprofitable to race geldings. The war was over by the time the next Derby Day rolled around and the rule was never enforced.

Late in 1918, Downs management formed itself into the Kentucky Jockey Club, Incorporated, a holding company for Churchill, Latonia, Douglas Park and Lexington, with Johnson N. Camden, an influential Woodford County horse breeder, State Senator and former member of the Kentucky State Racing Commission, serving as president.

A colt named Sir Barton swept three 1919 spring races — the Kentucky Derby, the Preakness at Pimlico and the Belmont in New York — which sportswriter Charles Hatton dubbed the Triple Crown. The name was lifted from a series of stakes races Johnson Camden had proposed for Lexington, Louisville and Latonia in 1912.

The following year, Man o' War's owner passed up the Derby. Samuel Riddle thought the early May date too taxing for the three-year-old colt, but ran him in the Preakness and Belmont. Man o' War suffered only one defeat in his incredible career and that was to H. P. Whitney's Upset which lost the 1920 Derby by a head to a brown gelding named Paul Jones.

Once peace returned and the influenza epidemic ran its course, Derby Day became big business. Working hand in hand with reporters, local investors and the mighty L&N Railroad, Winn made the Downs a mecca for celebrities and racing fans. When the 50th Derby rolled around in 1924, Winn asked Lemon & Son jewelers to create special trophies for the Derby, the Oaks, and the Grainger Memorial Stakes. Grainger had died five weeks before the 1923 Derby. The Oaks and Grainger Memorial trophies were challenge cups, massive lidded sterling pieces with silver horsehead handles, on which the winner's name was inscribed each year. The cups varied only in the style of the finials on the lids — an acorn for the Oaks trophy and a globe for the Grainger.

Winn presented the first Lemon & Son 14k gold Derby trophy to dowdy, dignified Rosa Hoots, owner of Black Gold, an animal whose career was so breathtaking and unbelievably heartbreaking that Hollywood scriptwriters' embellishments would only tarnish it in the screen story. Winn described Mrs. Hoots, wealthy widowed heir to her husband's Oklahoma oil fortune, with distant kinship ties to that state's Native American tribes, as a "simple aboriginal woman," conjuring up images of feathers and wigwams dear to American hearts. It was pure hype, all part of growing Derby mystique.

Publicity — getting the right people to the track and showcasing them — was Winn's key to success. He courted the press whom Clark had repeatedly antagonized. "Give me the five best writers in New York on my side, and you can have the rest," he said. Newspapers printed Derby stories as fast as Winn could make them happen. The Preakness and the Belmont might produce champions, but only the Derby produced legends.

For the 51st Derby, Winn went all out. Camera crews had long since cranked out film for movie houses but Winn wanted the Derby on nationwide radio as well. The first network play-by-play of a Derby was almost broadcast from one of the spires on May 16, 1925. Louisville radio station WHAS employees lugged their equipment up five flights of steep, spiraling stairs to the lookout that balmy spring day. Within an hour of the race, the weather changed dramatically. At post time a storm hit south Louisville, the likes of which spectators had seldom experienced. High winds stirred up track dust, then hail and a torrential downpour flooded the Downs. Ensconced in a spire, WHAS's elegant, silver-tongued announcer, Credo Harris, held on for dear life as the storm threatened his perch as well as his broadcast. There was no way to call a race he couldn't see. Flying Ebony made it safely to the finish line, but no winner's circle photo of him exists, the last lapse in a Derby tradition that began in 1906. From then on, broadcasting took place closer to the ground. Winn got a celebrity, New York Mayor Jimmy Walker, to present the Derby trophy in 1927. People were certainly more dependable than the weather!

Early in 1928, the Kentucky Jockey Club was dissolved and reformed, with the same Board of Directors, as the American Turf Association, a holding company chartered in the tax-free state of Delaware. The KJC operated four tracks in Kentucky and three in Illinois. Industrialist Samuel Culbertson assumed the presidency of Churchill Downs.

Then the world fell apart. The Crash of '29 would not affect racing at all, a local sportsman predicted early in 1930. He was wrong as wrong could be. Winn entertained the 17th Earl of Derby at the mid-May race that year, the first time a public address system was used at the Downs. Lord Derby presented the gold cup to millionaire William Woodward, Sr. whose Gallant Fox won for the prestigious, Maryland-based Belair Stud. It was strictly royalty and riches, just what the country needed to reassure itself that its economic woes would be short-lived.

The 1933 Derby was spiced by a stretch scuffle between the jockeys riding Head Play and Brokers Tip (named for Lexington food broker Mack Wood, who knew the tricks of the trade to cure sour horses) in a field of 13 entrants. Few spectators realized what had happened until *The Courier-Journal* front-paged a head-on shot of the horses the next day. Film of the "fighting finish" was shown in movie theaters around the world. These were hard times. Brokers Tip owner, gambler E. R. Bradley, held annual fund drives to benefit Bluegrass orphanages. All but the most die-hard Protestant denominations accepted his help.

By the fall of 1933, Winn's characteristic optimism was waning. He wrote Daingerfield: "Racing conditions are worse than I have ever seen them. This great sport, which we both love so much, has reached a most critical stage and I am fearful of what the future holds. I would like to know what you think about the situation. Your point of view might differ from mine." That the letter began as a letter of condolence on the death of Daingerfield's son, makes it all the more poignant and grim. Winn was then in charge of three Kentucky tracks. He cancelled Fall Meets at the Downs in 1931, not rescheduling them until 1934. Then the Kentucky Association track closed, ending a century-old Bluegrass tradition. Latonia, near Cincinnati, was shut down two years later and the American Turf Association was dissolved.

A few personal fortunes were recession-proof. To retailer Marshall Field, or candy heiress Ethel Mars and her Milky Way Farms, the cost of getting a Thoroughbred to the Derby presented no problem. Wealthy stable owners filled Derby fields throughout the 1930s, reassuring patrons in dime movie houses that prosperity was just around the corner. By 1938, Winn, newly appointed president, as well as executive manager of Churchill Downs, Incorporated, was able to pay for a tunnel to the infield which was terraced to improve drainage and provide better accommodations for the overflow Derby crowds who paid 50 cents for infield admission. The project was undertaken partly as a result of the devastating 1937 Flood. For weeks that winter, the grandstand, homestretch and infield had been covered with water so deep a rowboat was the only way to get across the track.

As the Depression loosened its grip on the economy, Winn put $100,000 into new seating in 1939. The 1903 lace-curtained clubhouse was buried under a multi-layered grandstand where the press was always welcome. In 1940, over 600 passes went to reporters; another 300 went to newsreel and photo agency representatives, radio, telephone and telegraph company officials. The only problem the press and racing fans had was finding their way around the split-level, architectural crazy quilt Churchill Downs had become. Tom Young, the track superintendent — and member of the local Selective Service Board — made a bad situation worse by working out a seating system that omitted Section 8, the notorious term for an army discharge!

War in Europe hastened economic recovery in this country as Americans got back to work. Then, after Pearl Harbor, it threatened to take away the very crowds Winn had used track profits to accommodate. By February, 1943, it looked as if there would be no 69th Derby. The government had already shut down all non-essential recreational attractions, including Lexington's Keeneland Race Course. Winn's response was ingenious. He wrote out-of-town boxholders, asking them to purchase their tickets, but not attend. Only Louisvillians would be at the Derby, Winn assured the press. Taxi drivers were told to drop passengers within a mile of the track. In reality, that was as close as they ever got because of Derby traffic jams, but the thought of women, dressed in their racing finery, hoofing it to the Downs, was somehow courageously patriotic. 62,000 people watched Count Fleet win the first leg of his Triple Crown victory that day, at what was dubbed the "street-car Derby."

As America was drawn deeper into World War II, all forms of civilian travel were heavily restricted. Joseph Eastman, a good friend of Winn's, headed the Office of Defense Transportation. He had long since issued orders closing down racetracks. He asked Winn to suspend racing at the Downs. Winn pointed out that the L&N had provided no special cars for Derby-goers since 1941. The ODT asked for a list of all boxholders and advised them against attending the race. The ever-resourceful Winn suggested prominent out-of-town boxholders pay for their seats again so their tickets could be turned over to military personnel.

Winn made it up to the blue-bloods when he published his memoirs in 1945. Their names were all there. William Woodward, chairman of The Jockey Club, was fondly remembered as Will. The Whitneys, the Wideners, racing's iconoclastic young Alfred Gwynne Vanderbilt, the duPonts, Firestones, and Chryslers — he named them one by one, reminding readers what a power in American racing circles the immigrant grocer's son from Portland had become.

For the last three years of the war, the grounds were awash with uniforms. Had the government closed Churchill Downs, the Armed Forces might have mutinied. It was an ill wind that didn't blow things right for Colonel Winn! From 1941 on, Winn helped war efforts with his War Charity Days. Churchill's board of directors donated $50,000 to the Red Cross, making the presentation on Derby Day 1942. Salvation Army kettles and bell ringers were a fixture outside the track gates. That fall, the infield became a sea of green tents known as "Camp Winn." Soldiers from Fort Knox demonstrated the field capabilities of newly-developed Sherman tanks, which were then shipped to North Africa to face and defeat Rommel's Afrika Korps.

In 1943, the Holy Name Society needed a place to hold its annual spring Corpus Christi Procession — ceremonies that always drew a huge crowd. Archbishop Floersh contacted Winn, who had been first Grand Knight of the first Knights of Columbus Council in Louisville. That June the stands were packed with celebrants. Churchill Downs became, to quote Winn, "a crazy quilt with a soul." When the government took over Louisville's west end State Fair Grounds, the 1944 State Fair was held in the infield. Patriotically named Thoroughbreds popped up everywhere. Bymeabond, Air Sailor, Jeep, Fighting Step and Foreign Agent were standouts among the 1945 Derby starters — the only time the Derby was ever run in June.

That February, Winn postponed closing nominations for the Derby because of a government-ordered ban on racing. "As springtime advances," *The Thoroughbred Record*'s Neville Dunn wrote, "Kentuckians hope Colonel Winn will find some way to convince official Washington of the necessity for this truly American sports function to be held as usual." Dunn then explained how Bluegrass horsemen could walk their Thoroughbreds the 80 miles from Lexington in Louisville in five days — a caravan unheard of in modern times, he called it — but not too difficult if it saved the Derby.

Winn no doubt held his breath when news of the Normandy invasion reached him. A postponed Derby once every century he could accept, a cancelled Derby never! The Germans surrendered on May 8, 1945. Winn cashed 155 nomination checks and ran a 16-horse Derby field on June 9, 1945. In the winner's circle, valet Andy Phillips threw one of Mrs. Kingsley Walker's rose garlands over Hoop Jr. and handed Covington-born jockey Eddie Arcaro five dozen long-stemmed roses. It was owner Fred Hooper's first try for Derby gold. For once, the favored Calumet entry ran second.

After the war, the 83-year-old Winn was busier than ever, managing racetracks in New York, Maryland and Illinois. Assault, Jet Pilot and Citation — Derby winners in '46, '47 and '48 — continued to remind racegoers how deeply World War II had changed their lives. The man whose trademarks were a smile and a big cigar had one final challenge, probably the most annoying of his career. In 1939, Warren Wright's Calumet Farm moved into racing like a juggernaut, mowing down opposition nationwide. Wright, with his Calumet Baking Powder fortune and his Texas oil interests, had the wherewithal to keep on racing throughout the war. His horses always had shoes, even when civilians did without. Gas rationing never kept Calumet's red and blue horse van in the garage. Unlike his father, Warren Wright was not a horseman. What he liked most about racing was being in the winner's circle. His secretary had standing orders not to accept challenge trophies, such as the Preakness' Woodlawn Vase, that had to be returned at the end of the year.

"The man who spends the most should win the most," Jockey Club member Wright declared. Nobody dared challenge his trainers, Ben and Jimmy Jones, a wily father and son team from Missouri, when they filled whole barns with Calumet horses and spread them out across the track like a phalanx during morning workouts. A juggernaut operation like Calumet did not serve racing well. Too much money went into one big pocket, driving smaller stables out of business. It depressed wagering because horses trained by the same trainer always ran as a single entry, which meant less profit for the track. By 1948, Wright already had two Derby trophies. With the Coaltown-Citation entry he was sure to have a third.

Winn was hardpressed to fill the 1948 Derby. The 109 nominations dwindled to six entries, the smallest Derby field since 1907. No one wanted to challenge the dynamic duo, who cinched their 1-2 victory by drawing the inside post positions — the shortest distance around the track. The 1948 Derby was a match race between two horses owned and trained by the same stable. Without vigorous Derby wagering, track profits plummeted to near-Depression levels. Winn was not happy with Calumet.

1949 was Churchill's 75th anniversary. The Derby was one of the few American races that had been run every year, over the same track, since its beginning. With 14 well-bred horses going to the post, the Diamond Jubilee Derby appeared to be a wide-open race. Ponder was the Calumet entry — a 16-1 longshot the Jones boys said couldn't outrun a Shetland pony. They were just in town, "Plain Ben" told reporters, for old times' sake. Ponder won by three lengths.

Then the most peculiar thing happened. The guard responsible for escorting Warren Wright to the winner's circle led him up a blind alley in the grandstand. A second guard led Wright to a dead end and the third guard got the thoroughly-confused Wright to the winner's circle long after Winn had presented the $10,000 diamond-horseshoed gold cup to Ben Jones. Maybe it was just a coincidence. If Winn had a hand in the mix-up, he never let on.

It was Winn's last Derby and he was an innovator to the end. WAVE, the 41st television station in the country, did a live on-site telecast of the Derby under the direction of veteran newsman George Patterson. Viewers around Louisville, where there were no more than 300 TV sets, and people as far away as Lexington and Paducah, saw, as well as heard, Matt Winn on the air, promoting the race he had turned into an international event. In his white suit, Winn was Kentucky's Colonel long before restaurateur Col. Harland Sanders came on the scene.

After his wife's death in 1912, Winn never remarried. Once his daughters were grown, his Louisville home was a suite of rooms at the track. Together with Tom Young, Winn planned every inch of the facility to please racing fans. Winn could be seen, even when he was in his 80s, on the grounds, sitting and cogitating before ordering the never-ending improvements, frontside and backside.

His daily luxuries were big, black cigars and a chauffeur-driven Duesenberg. Churchill's Irish Colonel appreciated good bourbon in moderation. When he handed drinks to friends, especially the younger ones, he was known to comment: "Some of the best men I ever knew tried to beat that stuff and lost. So be careful and don't let it lick you." Winn was a vigorous man who experienced radiant good health all his life. This he attributed to his habit of drinking the juice of two lemons every day — and having very long-lived parents. But the years eventually took their toll. By 1949, Winn knew that, short of a miracle, the Diamond Jubilee Derby would be his last. He died October 6, 1949, following two rounds of surgery at Louisville's St. Joseph's Infirmary.

For a man born during the Civil War, Winn had done what few would attempt. He guided Churchill Downs through the shadow of bankruptcy, politics, World War I, the Great Depression, a flood and World War II. From a grocer's wagon in the infield to television, Winn had seen the world change. He was one of a kind. No one of his stature was at hand to step into his shoes.

Chapter Eight

Winn's Legacy

When the board appointed New York sportswriter Martene Windsor "Bill" Corum — the United States Army's youngest Major in World War I — president, it was the first time the track's leader was neither a Kentuckian nor a horseman. Directors may have followed Winn's dictates in making their choice. He had always courted the New York press and made his apartment in the Waldorf Towers their home-away-from-home when he was in New York.

Corum's lasting contribution to the Derby was nicknaming it "the run for the roses," an expression Churchill Downs, Inc. has since trademarked. Other than that, Corum's was truly an absentee landlordship. He remained with Hearst publications, taking a two-month "vacation" from mid-March until after Derby to preside at the track. The first time Winn's valet awakened him at the crack of dawn for backside rounds, Corum was much taken aback. He confessed to getting home from New York clubs at sunrise, but he didn't know people who went to bed before they got up that early!

From 1950 to 1958, the track ran under its own steam; the days of innovative management were at an end. There was no Derby TV coverage again until 1952. Such was Corum's indifference that he gave his years as Churchill's president short shrift in his autobiography; to him, Louisville racing was an inconvenience that interfered with his sport of choice — boxing. In the absence of other sports and wagering opportunities, the Derby was so successful that the Downs, manned by a skeleton crew, could afford to drift from year to year.

There was great racing during those years, with the 1955 battle between Swaps, the California budget colt owned and trained by men who slept in his stall, and Nashua, royally bred scion of millionaire William Woodward, Jr.'s Belair Stud, being the most exciting contest of them all. In a race that made history, Swaps won the Derby, then lost a match race to Nashua the following August. After young Woodward's wife shot and killed him, claiming she thought he was a burglar, prominent Lexington horseman Leslie Combs bought Nashua from Woodward's estate for a syndicate bid of $1,251,200 — then the highest price ever paid for a stallion.

After Corum's death, retired Schenley Distillery president, Wathen R. Knebelkamp, served as Churchill Downs' president from 1959 to 1969. A highly respected Louisvillian, as well as a third-generation Thoroughbred owner whose father raced horses in two 1930s Derbys, the affable, charming Knebelkamp devoted himself to the Downs, reconnecting the track to Louisville and the Commonwealth. Knebelkamp encouraged the Louisville Area Chamber of Commerce to grow with the Derby. During Knebelkamp's presidency, the Derby Festival and the Pegasus Parade came into their own.

Tragically, the 1968 Derby was marred by an incident that those who knew Knebelkamp say broke his heart and may have hastened his death the following year. Racing officials claimed the winner, Dancer's Image, tested positive for an anti-inflammatory drug commonly known as "bute," then prohibited by the Kentucky Racing Commission. Peter Fuller, the straight-arrow New Englander who owned Dancer's Image, denied the charge. Later he suggested his colt had been drugged because of his pledge of support for Coretta King, widow of just-slain Nobel Prize winner, Dr. Martin Luther King, Jr., who had led a sit-in at the Downs' parking lot on Oaks Day the year before.

The 1967 demonstration had been part of a deeply disquieting spring. Five young men were arrested four days before the Derby after they raced down the stretch in front of horses in the first race. The Derby Festival's Pegasus Parade was cancelled and when Gov. Ned Breathitt assigned the National Guard to the Downs on Derby Day, Louisville looked as if it were under siege. After maintenance staff refused to cross King's picket lines, office staff worked through the night to clean up Oaks Day debris before Derby Day visitors arrived. The task was a monumental one, about which bitter feelings linger to this day.

So convoluted and bizarre was veterinarians' and sportswriters' testimony in the Dancer's Image case that it dragged on for several years. Finally the Kentucky Racing Commission declared that, except for pari-mutuel wagering, Calumet Farm's second place finisher, Forward Pass, was the 1968 Derby winner. Thus Warren Wright's widow, Lucille — by then married to Hollywood playboy Admiral Gene Markey — added an eighth Derby trophy to Calumet's already overflowing trophy room.

Lynn Stone was the track's president from 1970 to 1984. Racing, still unchallenged by other recreational opportunities, was never more exciting. In 1973, Secretariat, an extraordinary Virginia-bred colt, blazed across the finish line in record-breaking 1:59 2/5 time under jockey Ron Turcotte. It was a second, back-to-back Derby victory for C. T. Chenery, whose blue and white silks (colors of his beloved Lexington, Va., alma mater, Washington & Lee) had been worn by Riva Ridge the year before. The week after his 31-length Belmont victory, Secretariat made the cover of *Time, Newsweek,* and *Sports Illustrated.* In a year when Vietnam gripped Americans like a cold hand, and rumblings from a break-in at the Watergate Apartments led to President Nixon's resignation, the press voted Secretariat Horse of the Year, and Man of the Year. No one questioned their choice. Secretariat became the first of three horses to win the Triple Crown in the 1970s, a title unclaimed since Citation's 1948 sweep.

On the Derby's 100th Anniversary in 1974, a record-breaking crowd of 163,628 fans jammed the stands to watch Cannonade, a grandson of 1957 fourth place finisher Bold Ruler, win an emerald-encrusted gold Derby cup. A colt nicknamed "Baby Huey" because of his ungainly ways, took the Triple Crown in 1977 as Seattle Slew. With personable young trainer John M. Veitch and a home-bred named Alydar, Calumet's Lucille Markey made a final attempt to win the Triple Crown in 1978. Her colt ran second to Affirmed in all three races. Times were good. They didn't stay that way for long.

Lynn Stone retired just as burgeoning Big League sports began taking an ever-increasing bite of the public's time and pocketbook. Amidst declining profits and threats of hostile takeovers, Downs' board chairman Warner L. Jones, Jr., a Churchill descendent, 1953 Derby winner Dark Star's breeder, and owner of Hermitage Farm, brought in a new administrative team. Thomas H. Meeker, neither a Kentuckian by birth nor a horseman by choice, became the first United States Marine Corps Lieutenant Colonel to lead the corporation. Meeker's rank reflected his achievements as a highly-decorated officer in Vietnam. Prior to being named CEO, he was a partner in the Louisville law firm of Wyatt, Tarrant & Combs and Churchill's general counsel.

Meeker walked around the facility and didn't like what he saw. He focused on a Three-C program to rehabilitate the Downs — Capital Improvement, Community Relations and Customer Service. Grumpy, cigar-smoking pari-mutuel clerks were told to be friendlier to fans who wanted to back their faith in a horse with some hard-earned cash. Under Meeker's leadership, the facility, back- and frontside, underwent a 10-year, $35 million renovation that included renumbering all the seats so patrons no longer had to grapple with Tom Young's steadfast refusal to have a Section 8 at the Downs. Ground was broken for a turf course — named for Matt Winn — in 1985.

Under Kevin Nuss' direction, the infield has once again become a community gathering place for annual events such as the weekend-long June celebration of Kentucky crafts, and a Scout-O-Rama where youth members from the Lincoln Heritage Council, Boy Scouts of America, demonstrate scouting skills for 15,000 to 20,000 visitors.

In 1987, Churchill Downs, breaking with tradition, awarded the contract for the garland of roses to Kroger's, a Midwest grocery chain headquartered in Cincinnati. When local nurserymen with family ties to the Kingsley Walker family refused to sell roses to Kroger's, the grocery company announced plans to hybridize a special Derby rose. The rose garland once a simple shawl of roses and greenery, has grown apace. Today it is truly a blanket-sized tribute that envelopes the Derby winner. Kroger created a second floral tribute, the Lilies for the Fillies — a blanket of pink Stargazer lilies — for the winner of the Kentucky Oaks.

The Monday after the 1989 Derby, the racing world was confronted with a remarkably straightforward announcement. Thomas Meeker, on the recommendation of board chairman Jones, had taken temporary leave of his job to seek treatment for alcoholism. That same year, Churchill Downs, at the instigation of track lobbyist Paul McDonald, funded the Backside Project for Lifestyle Improvement, headed by Alliant Hospital psychologist Curtis Barrett. Bill Chenault, a former Thoroughbred owner, as well as a cousin of Overton Chenault, breeder of the 1901 Derby winner, was chosen as the program's on-site coordinator in 1989. Chenault's ancestors had come from Albemarle County, Va., and settled near Boonesboro in 1778, where, more than likely, they raced horses on the track there.

With grant money provided, in part, by Jim Ryan, a Maryland-based Thoroughbred owner and breeder, Churchill Downs and the University of Louisville co-sponsored the first annual Conference on Addictions in the Racing Industry. The August before the conference took place, Ryan had been expelled from The Jockey Club during its annual Saratoga meeting. He had incurred the wrath of

Jockey Club president Ogden Mills "Dinny" Phipps by suggesting that Jockey Club funds be used to provide counseling for those who needed help with addictive disorders. "Dinny" Phipps (for whose half-brother, Henry Ogden Phipps, the family had cancelled a race at Aqueduct the day after the 31-year-old Phipps died from an overdose of narcotics) deemed the health problems of people working with million-dollar Thoroughbreds not important enough to warrant an investment of The Jockey Club's resources. Jockey Club funds had to be conserved, as Phipps put it, "for a rainy day."

1989 had been a memorable year for "Dinny" Phipps, who was not a horseman like his steeplechase-riding mother, Lillian Bostwick Phipps, or his uncle, gentleman-jockey "Pete" Bostwick. Nor did he appear to have much in common with his petite, energetic grandmother, Mrs. Henry Carnegie Phipps (before her marriage, Gladys Livingston Mills), one of the most down-to-earth, astute judges of Thoroughbred horseflesh ever to grace American racing. Her Wheatley Stables' colt, Bold Ruler, had been the century's pre-eminent sire of Derby winners, including Secretariat. Oldtimers remembered when the elderly Mrs. Phipps took hold of Bold Ruler's lead shank on the way to Belmont's winner's circle and the capricious colt dropped his head and followed her like a barn pony. Phipps' Derby entry, Awe Inspiring, ran third to his father's Alydar-sired colt, press and betting favorite, Easy Goer. The Phipps' colts were soundly beaten by Arthur Hancock III's Stone Farm homebred, Sunday Silence, in both the Derby and the Preakness. Only Easy Goer's brilliant victory in the Belmont saved Phipps' family pride.

At the Breeders' Cup showdown in November 1989, Sunday Silence won again, further enhancing the reputation of Phipps' fellow Jockey Club member Hancock, whom an advisory trust headed by the senior Phipps had summarily dropped from Claiborne Farm management after the death of his father, A. B. "Bull" Hancock. Time had proven that Arthur Hancock's Virginia thoroughbred heritage, like that of his younger brother, Seth, and sister, Dell, was not to be denied.

When Thomas Meeker assumed the presidency of the Downs in 1984, the inaugural year of the Breeders' Cup, Thoroughbred breeding and racing was at its height. Two years later, Federal tax laws that wiped out hobby racing write-offs, coupled with the Middle East oil crisis, left the industry reeling. By 1989, a chain reaction of bankruptcies, indictments and trials, dispersals of major racing stables and precipitous drops in Thoroughbred foal registrations to their pre-1980 levels made headlines every week. A state lottery and the spread of casino gambling again challenged Kentucky racing as it had a century ago.

Today racing faces the same unresolved issues that confronted it in the 1890s. In 1992, Churchill's outspoken CEO was pilloried by industry leaders for alluding to them as "gnomes," a forthright assessment of each track's tendency to guard its own turf rather than work together. Racing executives solved the problem by shouting down the messenger rather than heeding the message and Meeker was forced to apologize. Since 1990, Churchill Downs has been increasingly expansionistic in its outlook. In 1991, it purchased the last harness racing track in Jefferson County, and, by 1992 — the year off-track betting was legalized in Kentucky — had converted it into Sports Spectrum, a state-of-the-art, inter-track wagering facility and training track. A harness racing track in Anderson, In., linked to off-site betting parlors, opened in September 1994, and held its first Thoroughbred race Sept. 1, 1995, with an Indiana Derby scheduled later in the fall.

The Kentucky Derby, still the first jewel of the Triple Crown, will be even more valuable in 1996 when the guaranteed purse is $1-million. Churchill Downs' board has committed itself to a $50- million makeover, both to upgrade the site and pave the way for casino gambling at the Downs, a course it is vigorously pursuing. Today the track's name and twin-spired logo are zealously guarded corporate trademarks which cannot be used, except in editorial context, without permission. Long gone are the days Matt Winn courted knick-knack makers whose wares publicized his beloved track.

When Churchill Downs celebrated its Twin Spires Centennial in 1995, two men on its management team were recognized for their contributions to the well-being of the industry. After widely broadcast pictures of game-to-the-end, broken-legged Thoroughbreds struggling valiantly to rise on three feet at New York's Belmont track led to public hue and outcry against the sport, Churchill Downs proved to be one of the safest tracks in America. Track superintendent Raymond "Butch" Lehr, Jr. has been at the Downs since he was a teenager, currying and tending the turf and dirt tracks as if people's and horses' lives depend on it — which they do.

On his 60th birthday, *Courier-Journal* sportswriter Jennie Rees called Downs' Director of Horsemen's Relations, Julian Logan

"Buck" Wheat, "Churchill's third spire." Wheat's ancestors imported horses into colonial Virginia. The Logans were among the earliest settlers in Paris, Ky. Years ago, Louisville Mayor Jerry Abramson dubbed Buck the "Mayor of the Backside." As an ambassador of goodwill, Wheat is without peer.

Mid-September, 1995, Churchill's backside work force and industry professionals were stunned to learn that Curtis Barrett had fired Bill Chenault, whose compassionate spirit and successful track record had brought him national recognition in the field of addictions counseling. With his leavetaking, another Churchill link to Kentucky racing history was severed.

Ignored by Churchill executives, as end-of-century gambling fever grips America, is the dismal 400-year history of what happens to racing when tracks become casino gambling sites. In 1994, Kentucky to the Front, a coalition funded by Churchill, Turfway Park, Ellis Park, the Red Mile (Lexington's harness racing track), Dueling Grounds Race Course (a steeplechase course and intertrack wagering site near the Tennessee border in Franklin, Kentucky) and the Kentucky Horsemen's Benevolent and Protective Association, spent over $300,000 to persuade legislators to put a constitutional amendment legalizing track-based casino gambling on the ballot.

Former Kentucky Governor, Julian Carroll, "ranting and raving like a revivalist preacher," *The Courier-Journal* editorialized, urged legislators to declare their belief in casino gambling. Neither Keeneland nor the Kentucky Thoroughbred Association supported Kentucky to the Front. Keeneland board chairman Ted Bassett, speaking with the knowledge that history repeats itself, quietly testified before the House Tourism Committee: "Keeneland feels casino gambling would be injurious, incompatible and injurious. . . It would seriously jeopardize the future of Thoroughbred racing in Kentucky." The Committee quickly agreed. The game was over, *The Courier-Journal* concluded, as least for the present.

Only one small piece of Winn's legacy remains unaccounted for. If you look at photographs of the Oaks trophy, you will see that the lid is topped by a globe and not an acorn. The whereabouts of the Grainger Memorial trophy, and the Oaks trophy lid, are mysteries only someone who reads this book may finally be able to explain.

Chapter Nine

Racing's Mighty Boys

When horses were few and far between, only the very wealthy rode. Common folk used ox-carts, or walked. The pastime of kings and courtiers was staghunting — a sport that filled their larders with tangy-tasting meat and kept them fit for war. Woe be unto the nobleman who didn't like "hawking, hunting and swift horse running."

After James I united England and Scotland in 1607, peace brought change. Freed from the burden of financing the border wars, England was able to expand her navy. Men got rich from commerce and international trade. With time on their hands, both men and women took to gambling, gaming and betting. Commoners, by law, were forbidden to race horses or bet. Gentlemen — aristocrats and army officers — were expected to gamble extravagantly.

Audiences who saw James Shirley's 1632 play, "Hyde Park," heard the hero, Jockey, say about a race he won: "The odds play'd bout my ears like cannon." Jockey, no doubt, was a gentleman by birth. But as stakes and wagers grew, any rider who could bring a horse home in front of the pack became a gentleman the second he was hoisted into the saddle and remained one until the race was over. Charles II was the last monarch to ride his own horses in races at Newmarket. Because of his equestrian skills, flat racing was dubbed "the Sport of Kings." His successor, William III, didn't ride, but he lavished money on race horses and lodging, food and clothing for 10 "riding boys," all supervised by William Tregonwell Frampton, a professional horse trainer whose royal title was "Keeper of the Running Horse." In less than a hundred years, the gentleman's hobby became a profession for jockeys and trainers alike.

Race tracks sprang up all around England. In the country, owners rode, or let friends jockey, their heavy, mixed-breed horses, which lumbered along for four to six miles at a pace that tested stamina, not speed. Spectators saw very little of the race, unless they followed along on horseback, or joined in what was usually a wild dash to the finish line.

Races were shortened as city crowds demanded action, speed and opportunities to bet. Owners hired jockeys with quick reflexes and aggressive ways, sometimes weighing as little as 55 pounds, to handle their high-strung Thoroughbreds. It was dangerous work, made more so by interference from spectators on the winding courses. At the 1776 Epsom Fall Meet a jockey was thrown, his foot caught in his stirrup, when a mounted racegoer crossed his path near the finish line. The horse dragged his rider to victory. Racing rules require the horse to carry full weight throughout the race. Nowhere does it say that the weight has to be in the saddle for the horse to win the race!

Weatherby's 1777 Racing Calendar advised track officials to make distance poles thin and brittle, after a boy called "Little Wicked" was cut to pieces on one of the heavy posts. The horse's owner reportedly cried over the loss of his "lad."

Wealthy English colonists brought their thoroughbreds and betting habits to America with them. Here, as in England, there were laws prohibiting tradesmen from racing or betting on horses. In a country so vast and thinly populated, men who smarted under aristocratic colonial rule simply went west to Kentucky or Tennessee, to establish more democratic racing, but jockey club members, just like their English counterparts, still controlled who rode and who didn't. Stewards could make jockeys exchange horses right before a race or allow owners to put their "boys" on the wildest, most savage mounts. More than one death on a racetrack was attributed to these arbitrary rulings, but jockeys had to do as they were told.

Jockeys were often slaves who lived in fear of offending their masters. Whether hired out to several horse owners or bound to one farm, a jockey's livelihood depended on staying on good terms with the stewards, so he accepted whatever punishment was handed out.

Racing always followed America's economic ups and downs, but war, especially the Civil War, took a terrible toll on men and horses, especially among Southern sympathizers in the Bluegrass. Horse breeders often gave their best horses to the Confederacy; or bands of marauders held farm owners at gunpoint while they helped themselves. On the other hand, the Civil War greatly expanded the reach of railroads and telegraph lines. With improved transportation and communication, new tracks opened and existing tracks became more accessible.

By the late 1870s, jockeys were America's sports heros. The best ones traveled cross-country by railroad, riding in California, Kentucky, St. Louis, New Orleans and the East. Some, like Indiana farmboy Tod Sloan and Lexington-born Isaac Murphy, were dandies who earned fabulous salaries and hobnobbed with the rich and famous. Others never made it that far.

On July 10, 1880 an obituary appeared in *The Thoroughbred Record*: "The colored jockey, Garrett Lewis, died at Hutchinson Station, Ky., on Monday, July 5th from internal injuries received in the mile heat race at St. Lewis, Mo. June 8th, in which he rode the chestnut gelding Bravo which stumbled, fell and threw Lewis, who was stunned severely. Afterwards he recovered enough to ride a few races at Chicago, Ill., but he had a relapse and died on his arrival home. He was a most excellent, obedient and good jockey and is a severe loss to the turf. He was in his eighteenth year." The obituary did not mention the May 18th victory on 1880 Kentucky Derby longshot Fonso that immortalized Garrett Lewis' name in racing history.

Almost without exception, riders such as Lewis grew up on horse farms and demonstrated a natural talent for riding at an early age. They were then turned over to trainers who, often as not, had been jockeys themselves when they were younger. There was an understanding that being a jockey, for those who survived the experience, was a phase of a lifelong career with horses. When they got too big to ride, they would join the ranks of trainers who developed horses for the boys that came after them. The system had worked that way for hundreds of years. After 1900, it never worked that way again.

The 1890s were the last golden decade for Kentucky-born jockeys. Those who had talent could name their price. Racing publications spoke out against the salaries paid riders, calling the young men "dictators of the track" for commanding annual retainers of $5,000 to $15,000 from fabulously wealthy horse owners. When 13-year-old "Soup" Perkins signed a $4,000 contract to ride for the Fleischmann Stable in 1893, the deal made headlines. He was the best-paid teenager in the country! Beyond his annual salary, Perkins got a percentage of each purse he won and could ride for other stables when Fleischmann Stable horses weren't running.

The 1890s saw gambling fever spread as it never had before. Bookmakers promoted wagering as a form of investment. Excess encouraged excess. At New York's Coney Island, trainer Bill Daly ran a jockey school for immigrants' children and boys he recruited from orphanages, promising to make riders out of them in five years. By the end of 1892, he had been arrested 15 times for beating his charges with baling sticks or horse whips — offenses for which he was never prosecuted. He disciplined his riders with a barrel stave and starved the ones who couldn't "make weight" by locking them up, without food, until the "problem" went away. "Father Bill"'s boys, schooled to be ruthless in the saddle, gradually replaced the more skillful and gentlemanly farm-trained Southern Black riders. Without ethics or loyalties, these newcomers were easily threatened and bribed. They abused their horses as badly as they were abused, freely applying whips and spurs to their exhausted mounts.

Racing was on a rough track, made rougher because of the 1890s recessions that bankrupted many prominent racing stables before the turn of the century. In the dog-eat-dog atmosphere that prevailed, Daly's boys were much in demand for their slick riding skills, then it was every man for himself as anti-gambling legislation closed tracks and forced horse owners to send their choice Thoroughbreds abroad or turn them into horsemeat.

Matt Winn kept Churchill Downs open during the years Eastern and Southern tracks were shut down. But by then, established jockeys, who had neither farm nor family ties to keep them in America, had long since gone to Europe. Danny Maher, a former Daly "boy" was reportedly earning $50,000 in England. Of 18 top American riders who emigrated, a third had had Derby mounts before 1905. All were living like kings with incomes in excess of $10,000.

The American invasion brought about changes, especially in British racing. English riders tended to save their horses for a fast and furious finish, so Jockey Club members who acted as stewards could see all they needed to see from their box near the finish line. American riders, they quickly noticed, rode every race vigorously from start to finish. It was suggested that turrets be built all around the tracks and stewards be paid to man them, as Jockey Club gentlemen could hardly be expected to leave their comfortable quarters and climb into these lookouts.

Between pressure from anti-gambling leagues and the rough element that controlled what few tracks were still in business, racing deteriorated so quickly in America that some tracks made an effort to restore the appearance of respectability by the token use of women stewards. One turfwriter even suggested that girl jockeys would be better riders than boys. "It may not be in our time," he concluded, "but women's position on the turf is by no means stationary, great as have been the strides it has taken in recent years."

Right before World War I, a jockey named Roscoe Ganz from Jeffersontown, Ky., pulled off the improbable feat of riding and winning his first Kentucky Derby in record time on Donerail, which went off at odds of $91.45 to $1. The payoff on a $2 bet was $180.90. Young Ganz changed his name to Goose because, with war at hand, Ganz was too German-sounding. He became known as the Golden Goose, both for his brilliant riding and his ability to invest the money he earned.

When his brother was killed in a riding accident, Goose worked with Lexington Thoroughbred breeder, E. R. Bradley, to develop protective headgear for riders. The first hard hat was no more than a leather bowl-shaped beanie riders were required to wear under their silk caps. Neither the cap nor the beanie was secured by a chin strap, but riders nonetheless resisted wearing the newfangled safety equipment. Tracks were forced to position a man armed with a stout stick at the door of the jockeys' room. He had orders to tap each rider on the head. Those who flinched were sent back for their hard hats.

Once 1920s prosperity revived racing, jockeys again became stars but it would be two decades before their real incomes reached the heights to which they had soared in the 1880s and '90s.

Brothers Mack and William Garner, Irishmen from Iowa, were Derby regulars at Churchill Downs from 1916 to 1944. Louisville-born Charlie "Flying Dutchman" Kurtsinger won the 1931 and 1937 Derbys. But the most famous jockey of them all was Earl Sande, a hard-drinking, hard-driving rider immortalized in sportswriter Grantland Rice's poem:

Maybe there'll be another, Heady and game and true-
Maybe we'll find his brother at drivin' them horses through.
Maybe-but, say, I doubt it, Never his like agin-
Never a handy guy like Sande, Bootin' them babies in!"

Sande dominated the Kentucky Derby in the 1920s, winning in 1923, 1925, and 1930. Ironically, Rice, who watched Sande win many a race, made no effort to meet Sande until years after the poem had become a classic.

Just as racing really got going again, the Great Depression destroyed fortunes and forced tracks and stables into bankruptcy. Once-wealthy men, faced with economic ruin, could not afford racing as a hobby. Jobs were scarce and jockeys fought for them, on the track and off. Eugene James' body was fished out of Lake Michigan weeks after he rode Burgoo King to victory in 1932. His murderer, if murder it was, was never found. The 1933 Derby in which Don Meade and Herb Fisher fought each other down the homestretch, wasn't the only incident of its kind, it was just the only one a daring photographer caught on film.

Two years later, during Churchill Downs' fall race meet, 20-year-old Derby winner Willie "Smoky" Saunders, who had ridden Omaha for William Woodward's Belair Stud that spring, was implicated in one of the grisliest murders Louisville had ever seen.

On October 20th, 1935, the mangled body of Evelyn Sliwinski was found on River Road near Blankenbaker Lane. According to an eye witness, the young woman, whom reporters coyly described as a "party girl," had been let out of Saunders' car in the city near Campbell and Broadway, then run down by Walter Schaeffer, the exercise rider who was driving Saunders' car. Saunders and another woman, both very drunk, were in the car when the "accident" happened. The two men put Mrs. Sliwinski back in the car and headed up River Road where they dumped their victim on to the pavement and ran over her body several times at high speed. Schaeffer fled in Saunders' car, but was apprehended in Baltimore. A coroner's jury blamed him for Sliwinski's death. Saunders was indicted as an accessory to the murder. Track officials asked him not to ride until he cleared himself.

At the January, 1936 trial, the other woman refused to testify and a Criminal Court jury acquitted Schaeffer. The judge had no choice but to drop the charges against Saunders. The jockey, reporters noted, clutched a rabbit's foot in his pocket as he heard the motion for dismissal. Saunders then headed for Florida where he rode for Lexington's Hal Price Headley, whose attorney had represented Saunders at the trial. Omaha was Saunders' first and only Derby mount. Many felt he had gotten away with murder. The affair did nothing to endear jockeys or attorneys to the public.

Making his debut several years later was a young rider from Covington, Ky., named Eddie Arcaro. He was a fearless fighter in the irons, but by then the newly developed patrol camera was recording races with an impartial, all-seeing eye. Early in his career, Arcaro received a year's suspension for rough riding.

"The patrol cameras made us honest," he commented many years later. Arcaro celebrated the first of five Derby victories in 1938. By the late 1930s, Depression era conditions on racetracks grew so bad, even fierce rivals were willing to band together just to survive.

In 1940, a group of New York riders, led by Sam Renick, formed the Jockeys' Guild, a national self-help organization for riders who chose to join. Change came slowly, but surely.

In 1951, Conn McCreary, a jockey his peers thought was all washed up, won his second Kentucky Derby on long shot Count Turf. McCreary later told newsmen he wished he had a trophy to commemorate the victory. The Downs responded by having the gold Derby trophy recast in smaller silver versions, which were presented to the winning jockey and trainer for the first time the following spring. McCreary got his Derby trophy and the silver replicas have been a Derby tradition ever since.

By the 1960s, jockeys were once again among the best paid sports stars in the country, but it was still an all-male profession. It required a 1968 Circuit Court order to get Maryland to grant 28-year-old U. S. Equestrian Team Olympic rider Kathryn Kusner her jockey's license. Penny Ann Early became the second licensed female jockey when she was granted a temporary license by the Kentucky State Racing Commission two months later. She was scheduled to ride in a Fall Meet claiming race at Churchill Downs amid rumors that male jockeys were prepared to boycott in protest. When the track turned up muddy, her horse was scratched from the race. In February, 1969, 19-year-old Diane Crump became the first woman to ride in a pari-mutual race in North America, at Hialeah Park. Crump was 15th, riding Fathom for Louisvillian W. L. L. Brown in the 1970 Kentucky Derby. Crump made her way into the record books again when she returned to riding at age 47, chalking up her first victory at Turfway Park on Jan. 18, 1995, riding Celestial Halo. Crump is the first woman in Kentucky to be licensed as both a jockey and a trainer. Since 1970, only three other women, Patricia Cooksey, Andrea Seefeldt and Julie Krone have ridden in Derbys. Cooksey was the first woman to ride in the Preakness (1985) and Krone was the first woman to win the Belmont Stakes (1993).

State Racing Commission stewards, like officers of old-time jockey clubs, still control decisions about licensing or suspending riders. But jockeys, through their Guild, have more say-so over the conditions under which they work and ride. Gone are the days when a jockey could be ordered on an unmanageable horse or face a poorly maintained track without recourse.

Perils remain, nonetheless. From 1960 through 1991, an average of 2.5 jockeys died on racetracks every year. Dozens more were injured or paralysed in racing spills. Increased use of lightweight safety equipment and growing concern about equine breakdowns appear to have made a significant difference in jockeys' mortality and injury rates. Still, on the average, a jockey stays in the profession less than two years. It is not just injury, but the stress of maintaining riding weight, coupled with a nomadic lifestyle, that challenges the would-be professional. Only a select few men and women ride successfully for more than a decade. Only a handful continue to ride into their 40s.

Ounce for ounce, a jockey must be the fittest of all athletes. Balanced on a thousand-pound animal, riding stirrup to stirrup where misjudging fractions of an inch can be fatal, the rider must be a superb horseman. Weight requirements are just as challenging today as they ever were. A horse ridden by an apprentice jockey, called a "bug boy" because of the * before his name in the program, will start out carrying 10 pounds less than a fully licensed rider. The weight allowance serves as an incentive for trainers to use a newcomer, because the less weight a horse carries, theoretically, the faster he can run. After winning a set number of races, the apprentice loses his "bug" and becomes a journeyman (professional) jockey who must ride at the assigned weight.

Few full-grown men, regardless of their height, can keep their weight within the 100 to 110 pounds required to compete effectively. Years ago, riders resorted every known trick to keep weight off. Before the days of the sauna-like "hot box," jockeys submerged themselves in manure piles, hoping heat from the rotting compost would melt them down to size. When racing was seasonal, the better jockeys, whose incomes allowed them to eat well all winter, found themselves in no shape to make weight in the spring. Starvation dieting was called "wasting" and more than one famous rider is known to have wasted himself to an early grave. Battling the bulge by "flipping" — a pattern of eating and self-induced vomiting — leads to bulimia. When legendary Kentucky jockey Isaac Murphy died suddenly in February 1896, the cause of death was listed as pneumonia. More than likely, he had begun an all-to-common yearly ritual of eating and purging, dying from infection caused by vomit ingested into his lungs. Nowadays both Guild representatives and racetrack stewards monitor jockeys closely for signs of problems. Counseling is available for those with eating and addictive disorders.

Riding is a complex business as well as a perilous profession. Successful jockeys are represented by agents who negotiate every morning with trainers for the mounts their clients will ride that afternoon. Winners get 10% of the owner's percentage of the purse, second place and third place finishers get 5%. Also-rans are paid a standard fee, usually $40. Riders are self-employed. From their earnings they must pay for tack and clothing, the services of a valet and agent, plus living and travel expenses. Compared with other professional athletes today, jockeys' earnings are not high. In 1994, the average jockey earned approximately $25,000 — not a lot for taking your life in your hands, six or seven times a day.

Kentucky State University Archives

Isaac Murphy

Chapter Ten

Black Legends of the Bluegrass

For centuries, probably since time began, there has been a camaraderie among horsemen, regardless of their rank or color. Managing high-strung Thoroughbreds was a prestigious job in the South, where everything depended on keeping a horse fit to run — and win. Successful farms were team efforts. Those who planned equine matings were the geneticists of their day. Farriers and blacksmiths were nature's design engineers and mechanics. Grooms were pharmacists and midwives to their charges.

Throughout the 1700s and 1800s, the most successful stables were located in Kentucky, Tennessee, Virginia, Maryland, the Carolinas and Alabama. No plantation owner stayed in business very long without the help of men who shared his passion for the sport. A love of horses couldn't be beaten into a slave. The heart, talent and skill came from within.

Long before English Thoroughbreds evolved from Arab and Hobby stock, West Africa developed a horse culture of its own. An extensive overland caravan trade existed between North and West Africa prior to the 1400s, when the Portuguese first sailed around Africa's western coast. West Africans traded gold, ivory, slaves and kola nuts for North African horses, textiles, books, swords and knives. As populations grew, the West African kingdoms began fighting among themselves. Every ruler maintained his own army, some with cavalry units of over 10,000 horses. By the 1600s, Portuguese slave traders were waiting at the docks to buy African prisoners-of-war whom West Africans traded for European goods, New World rum and Arab horses.

English aristocrats founded Jamestown in 1607. The first horses that didn't end up in settlers' stew pots were bred in Virginia the same year Africans slave ships arrived, 12 years later. Southern plantation owners had "droit de seigneur," literally the right to rape their slaves and indentured servants. If a female caught the plantation owner's eye, she was his for the taking. Children "of color" grew up alongside their white half-sisters and -brothers.

Boys learned how to take care of horses before they were allowed to ride. If they were good riders, their professional careers began when they were 10 or 11 years old and weighed between 55 and 75 pounds. Before the Civil War, America's top riders were, or had once been, slaves. Racing was a dangerous sport. Until it was obliterated to make way for a subdivision in 1994, there was a cemetery at the edge of Woodlawn Race Course where Black jockeys who died at the site were buried.

Those who survived usually got too big to ride by their late teens. Depending on their talents, they became grooms, trainers or stud managers. Right after the Revolution, the most famous Southern trainer was Austin Curtis, who had been North Carolina quarter horse breeder Willie Jones' jockey. Jones' nephew, Allen Jones Davie, himself a well-known horseman, wrote about Curtis: "The certificate as to the blood of Mr. Marmaduke Johnson's old Medley mare should be taken by the public as satisfactory on that subject — because the blood was so stated by Austin Curtis (who purchased the mare for Mr. Johnson) and who, although a man of color, was one on whom all who knew him relied. Austin was a freed man of my family, and he gave me the pedigree at a time when I contemplated buying a brood mare of the stock."

Charles Stewart was probably the best known trainer in the ante-bellum South. Stewart's reminiscences, published after the Civil War, tell of his travels as exercise boy, jockey, trainer and stud groom for Marmaduke Johnson's son, Col. William Ransom Johnson, the "Napoleon of the Turf." They make for interesting reading. Stewart enjoyed negotiating deals for his freedom. He would bargain for a fabulous price for himself, then, right before the agreement was signed, tell the purchaser the deal was off because he preferred being Col. Johnson's slave. Stewart was ruthless — he sold his own wife and children into slavery — but his integrity as a horseman was never questioned.

Slaves could earn their freedom on the track. Cato (pronounced Cate-o), who rode Wagner in the 1839 match race against Grey Eagle at Louisville's Oakland Course, became a free man after he won the first heat.

Captain Willa Viley, owner of the great Thoroughbred Lexington, purchased a trainer named Harry for $1,500. Viley freed him and paid him $500 a year for the rest of his life to train his horses. Kentucky was a slave state whose statutes, by the 1840s, required freed slaves to leave the state, but Viley ignored the law and did as he pleased.

Freemen lived side by side with slaves such as George, whose owner advertised in the June 19, 1827 *Louisville Daily Focus*: "$50 Reward for yellow fellow named George — 5' 10" tall — a blacksmith by trade — escaped from steamboat Lexington." Slaves bound for the Deep South were chained together and driven to the auction block along the same streets racegoers used in Lexington. Louisvillians going to Woodlawn Race Course in 1860 — where Blacks paid 50 cents for admission — passed the notorious Arterburn slave pens on First Street, but Blacks and whites mingled freely at Louisville and Lexington tracks.

Both before and after the Civil War, Ansel was the best known trainer in the country. He first made national headlines in Alabama in 1855 as the trainer of a fabulous distance horse named Brown Dick; then Lexington Thoroughbred owner Keene Richards bought Ansel and brought him to Kentucky. When Richards lost his fortune, Richards' friend, Robert A. Alexander — the wealthiest Thoroughbred breeder in the state — purchased Ansel, freed him, and put his best horses in Ansel's hands. After R. A. Alexander died, Ansel went to work for H. Price McGrath, a Versailles, Ky., tailor-turned-gambler rich enough to buy a Lexington horse farm he renamed McGrathiana and build a mansion that looked like Saratoga's United States Hotel. The same day Meriwether Lewis Clark announced plans for a new track in Louisville, newspapers carried a long interview with "Uncle" Ansel, who was then in New York with McGrath's top runner, Tom Bowling.

McGrath was an obnoxious man. He wore wide-brimmed white hats and bright red neckties, talked about his "darkies" as if they were still slaves, ran his horses into the ground, and threw lavish burgoo and bourbon parties at McGrathiana Stud. His favorite jockey, Bobby Swim, was a braggart and cheat. Even turf writers breathed a sigh of relief when Swim, who won the 1876 Derby on Vagrant, died young. Ansel put Oliver Lewis, an experienced Black jockey, on Aristides with good reason. Fourteen of the 15 riders in that first Kentucky Derby were topnotch Black riders; William Lakeland, an Englishman, was the only white jockey in the group.

After that race, a reporter described Ansel as a "gray haired old gentleman of color, stout and hearty as oak, who, being a true Christian, neither drank, cussed nor gambled." Ansel not only won the Derby, he was the track's leading trainer that spring. He eventually left McGrath and worked for Gen. Abe Buford, until senility forced him to retire. Sixty years after that first Derby, Churchill Downs gave Ansel a new name — A. Anderson. When he died in 1881, *The Thoroughbred Record* printed his obituary and his last name — Williamson. Ansel Williamson, 75 years old, had trained horses until two years before his death. He and Keene Richards, his old master, were friends to the end, the obituary noted. It is ironic that Ansel, who was such a fixture at Saratoga every summer, is not in Saratoga's National Museum of Racing Hall of Fame.

Other boys Ansel trained were Henry Overton, R. A. Alexander's well-known stud groom, and Edward Dudley Brown, the fleet-footed jockey Ansel nicknamed "Brown Dick" after his fastest Thoroughbred. Robert A. Alexander purchased eight-year-old Ed Brown at the Lexington slave market in 1858. By the time Brown was 16, he was one of the top jockeys in the country; by age 22 he had outgrown the saddle. From 1874 on, Brown trained a long string of national champions, including 1877 Kentucky Derby winner Baden Baden for Daniel Swigert, for whom he rode 1870 Belmont Stakes winner, Kingfisher. Brown was leading trainer at the Louisville Jockey Club eight times during the 1870s and 1880s. His record in Lexington and the East is equally impressive.

At the 1894 Saratoga yearling sales, Brown and his white partner, H. Eugene Leigh, bought a colt they named Ben Brush after the superintendent of the Gravesend track in Brooklyn, New York. Ben Brush won nine big races as a two-year-old, then Mike Dwyer, a weathy Brooklyn butcher, bought Ben Brush for $25,000 and won the 1896 Kentucky Derby with him. Next, Brown bought, trained, and sold John E. Madden the 1898 Kentucky Derby winner, Plaudit. Madden, a product of the Pennsylvania coal fields, was an outstanding athlete, loyal friend and fearless opponent, whether the opposition was horse or human. By spring 1899, Brown was Madden's associate. At the bottom of the newspaper page where the notice of M. Lewis Clark, Jr.'s suicide appeared, was a note: "John E. Madden has shipped most of his stable from Louisville to Westchester. He left his Derby candidates at Louisville in "Brown Dick"'s charge."

In 1895, *The Thoroughbred Record* stated: "Brown Dick is one of the richest colored men in Kentucky, being worth $75,000 surely and $100,000 probably, with nearly all his assets in cash." At his death in 1906, he was almost broke. "He has been generous and is known to have aided white friends as generously as Negroes. He has lost many thousands of dollars in loans to turfmen and trainers," a *Lexington Herald* reporter wrote. Through hard times, Brown had kept faith with members of his own profession. It is no wonder that his son recalled how hundreds of Louisvillians dropped what they were doing and came to pay their respects when he died. When Edward Dudley Brown was inducted into the Racing Hall of Fame in 1984, *The Blood-Horse* called him "one of the most celebrated trainers of any era."

William Walker, the dean of American pedigree experts at the time of his death in 1933, was Brown's closest friend and one of the few men who ever got the best of Louisville Jockey Club President M. Lewis Clark. Walker's obituary stated he was born a slave in 1860 on the Woodford County Nantura Farm of John Harper — later home of the great horse Ten Broeck. Other accounts list his birthplace as Abe Buford's Bosque Bonita Farm, where Walker got his start as a jockey. Walker was 11 when he rode his first race at Jerome Park in New York. He rode his first winner in Lexington before he turned 12 and was a stakes-winning jockey by age 13. He rode the fourth and eighth place finishers in the 1875 and 1876 Kentucky Derbys, then won the 1877 Kentucky Derby on Baden Baden.

At the first Spring Meet, Clark and the Louisville Jockey Club commended him for bravery after he kept the horse he was on from breaking through the outside rail and mowing down spectators in front of the grandstand. He was also given $50 for being "best-behaved jockey on the grounds" that year. Walker's run-in with Clark at the Ten Broeck-Mollie McCarthy Match Race in 1878 was the first time a jockey publicly contradicted a member of a jockey club or a track president as powerful as Clark. Two weeks after the race, Walker got to tell his side of the story to a Cincinnati reporter who was out to discredit Clark any way he could. *The Thoroughbred Record* promised readers that, having aired the truth of the matter, they wouldn't mention it again. Clark, in other words, was not entitled to a rebuttal.

Walker's career as a jockey lasted 25 years. He retired shortly after he rode The Winner to a seventh place finish in the 1896 Derby. By then, he had enough money to buy a three-story townhouse on South First Street, a reporter from *The Indianapolis Freeman* described as "brilliant and richly furnished," but Walker was seldom home to enjoy the decor. He was a respected pedigree expert, able to recite Thoroughbred genealogies from memory. What was more important, he knew which stallions should be bred to which mares to produce top-notch runners. John E. Madden was Walker's biggest client and many a Hamburg Place champion resulted from Walker's knowledge of what are called "nicks," the pedigrees that balance and enhance each other. When Madden announced the dispersal of his breeding stock in 1918, a whole new generation of Bluegrass horse-man waited on "Uncle Bill" to give sales and matings his stamp of approval. After Madden died, Walker, in spite of arthritis, made the summer trek to the Saratoga Sales alone, and worked as a clocker at Churchill Downs, recording early morning workouts for the *Daily Racing Form*. Walker and his wife, Hannah, had no children. Today they lie forgotten, buried in unmarked graves in a cemetery not far from the track.

Dudley Allen, a power in Bluegrass racing circles, was the first Black to own and train a Derby winner — 1891 betting favorite, Kingman. Allen also trained 1876 Derby winner, Vagrant, but Churchill Downs credits that win to William Backhouse Astor's trainer, in spite of a 1891 post-Derby *Courier-Journal* interview in which Allen pointed to Kingman's stall and remarked "That's a lucky stall. It was in that very same place that I trained Vagrant for the Derby."

Long before 1891, Dudley Allen was a partner in several rac-ing ventures, including Jacobin Stable. Allen purchased Kingman as a yearling from his Tennessee breeder and, at Georgetown business-man Kinzea Stone's insistence, sold Stone half interest in the colt. Stone's descendants inherited the silk purse that held Kingman's Derby winnings. It was eventually sent to the Kentucky Derby Mu-seum with a letter stating that the Jacobin Stable alias was used to conceal the names of the partners, because Allen was a Negro and such business arrangements were frowned on. They had not read *The Courier-Journal*'s day-after-Derby race review headlined "DUDLEY ALLEN'S IDEAS — The trainer of the Winner Tells How His Pet Won the Big Race." Dudley Allen died in Lexington in 1911, ending a successful career that spanned 40 years.

Isaac Murphy, "Kingman's Great Rider", as *The Courier-Journal* called him, was pictured along with his post-race wrap-up of the event. Murphy, the paper noted, "is the wealthiest jockey on the turf. His income has ranged from $10,000 to $15,000 for over five years. He lives in Frankfort [sic] when not with the races and when at home devotes his time to study and reading. His reputation for hon-esty and integrity is a matter of great pride among turfmen and they never lose the opportunity to boast of his qualities, both as a horse-man and a man. The great rider is only 27 years of age but he has been a conspicuous figure on the turf since he was a mere boy."

In 1891, Murphy was a tarnished legend making a comeback from his heartbreaking 1890 season. By the 1960s, it took two years to locate his grave. The woman who began the search for Isaac Murphy was Keeneland librarian Amelia Buckley. After she read a newspaper account stating that Murphy was buried in New Orleans, she called Frank Borries, a Lexington writer and racing historian. Borries eventually tracked down a man who lead him to a concrete shaft in the rear of the Number Two African Cemetery on the north side of Lexington's East Seventh Street. The monument was col-lared in red, with a white diamond in the center. There were two such monuments then standing in the cemetery.

On May 4, 1967 — the day before Martin Luther King's Oaks Day demonstration at the Downs — Miss Buckley, the Borries family and a host of Lexington's civic leaders unveiled a large gran-ite memorial at Murphy's new resting place in Man o' War Park at Faraway Farm. In Lexington, burying Kentucky's best rider next to Kentucky's most famous horse made good sense. Today they rest at the entrance to the Kentucky Horse Park. In sculpture and stone, their monuments remind visitors what the Commonwealth is all about.

Frank Borries' widow became Murphy's biographer and cus-todian of Murphy's original tombstone. In 1991, Betty Borries do-nated it to the Kentucky Derby Museum where it is exhibited today. Since the 1980s, every project concerned with the African Ameri-can contribution to Thoroughbred racing has benefited from the ef-forts of their son, Phil von Borries, to retrieve the long-overlooked records of Black horsemen.

Isaac Burns Murphy didn't die unremembered. He was bur-ied on a snowy, February Sunday, five days after his death on Feb. 12, 1896. Over 500 mourners took part in the funeral procession, the second largest in Lexington's history. A memorial to Murphy, writ-ten by L. P. Tarleton and Tarleton's Black trainer, "Uncle Eli" Jor-dan, was published in *The Thoroughbred Record* a month after he died.

Murphy was born Jan. 1, between 1858 and 1861, (Murphy listed various years) to James Burns, a Fayette County freeman. Burns, a bricklayer, enlisted in the United States Army and died at

Camp Nelson, outside Lexington. After the war, his widow and two small children lived with her father, Green Murphy, a well-known bell ringer and crier at Lexington auctions. The first yearling Murphy was hoisted aboard in 1873 threw him and he refused to get back on. Instead, he worked for two years as a groom at Fleetwood Farm, where Mrs. Tarleton educated him, turning him into one of the most eloquent spokesmen American racing has ever had. In January 1875, he was handed over to "Uncle Eli" again. By May, Isaac Burns was riding at the newly-opened Louisville Jockey Club track. Two seasons later, he was a standout at Saratoga. He had added "Murphy" to his name after winning his first race. For the next 10 years, Murphy rode horses Jordan — who tied for first place honors at Louisville's 1879 Spring Meet — trained.

Murphy not only brought extraordinary talent, dedication and an incredible sense of timing to his work, he was built like a horseman, with long arms, a compact torso and long legs. Murphy handled both horses and men with consummate ease. He always kept his word, never welshing on a contract, oral or written. He did not bet or swear or drink — until he began using champagne to suppress his appetite. He first rode at 87 pounds and would die, as many jockeys did, from the strain of trying to stay that size.

Unlike most American jockeys of his era, Murphy had no desire to ride in England, where the press nicknamed him "the Black Archer." (Turfwriters in this country responded by calling English jockey, Fred Archer, "the white Murphy.") Murphy's reasoning was sound. "It would be a disadvantage," he told reporters, "to any horse I rode, for they combine against our white jockeys over there and they would beat any horse I rode sure."

Murphy once saved a young white rider's life after other riders nearly pulled him off his horse during a race. Murphy himself told of going down with a horse when the horse in front of him fell. On the ground, Murphy was hit by another horse before he dragged the first horse's badly injured jockey to safety.

In March 1883, Murphy's ad appeared in *The Thoroughbred Record*: "I will make engagements to ride in the stakes for the coming racing season at Lexington, Louisville, Latonia, Chicago and Saratoga. I will be able to ride at 110 (possibly 107) pounds."

With an eye to the future, Murphy claimed his owner's colors — black jacket, red cuffs and white belt, red cap with green tassel — in 1888. By then he had married Lucy B. Murphy and was living in a towered townhouse on Third Street, from which he could look out over the Lexington Association track.

At the beginning of every racing season a Lexington reporter interviewed Murphy. From one of these articles, written in 1889, comes his often-quoted statement: "I am as proud of my calling as I am of my record and I believe my life will be recorded a success, though the reputation I enjoy was earned in the stable and in the saddle. It is a great honor to be classed as one of America's greatest jockeys." He became a Mason and joined the Knights Templar. In all things, Isaac and Lucy Murphy were pillars of the community.

Then the years of plenty started taking their toll. Murphy's weight skyrocketed every winter. A photograph shows the once-svelte Murphy with a paunch even loose silks didn't hide. In January 1890, Murphy got into a dispute with Ed Graves, a "gentleman rider," over who had the fastest colt at the sloppy Kentucky Association track. They agreed to a quarter-mile sprint which Graves, much to Murphy's chagrin, won by a head. Early in March, *The Lexington Leader* reported that Murphy weighed over 133 pounds but "expects no difficulty in reducing his weight to 112 before the racing season begins." Murphy rode Riley, his second Derby winner, at 118 pounds on May 14th. He had lost at least 16 pounds in nine weeks!

Then came the disastrous report, on Aug. 27, 1890, that Murphy had fallen off his horse, drunk, at the Monmouth Park track, the day before. Some turf writers blamed Murphy's disgraceful last place finish with James Ben Ali Hagan's mare — the betting favorite — on a champagne hangover. Murphy was suspended; any other rider would have been ruled off the track for life. Murphy claimed he had been poisoned, which, given the Clerk of Scales' statement that Murphy was perfectly sober before the race, was a mitigating factor in his sentencing. There was no question that by the end of the race Murphy was in tremendous pain. Later that year a Lexington reporter described Murphy's face as pinched and drawn. He was still under a New York doctor's care and spoke of an inflamed stomach on which he kept a bandage all the time. "I can't say definitely I was poisoned," he told the reporter, "but something suddenly got the matter with me and I have never been well since." He shows the unmistakable signs of having been a very sick man, the reporter concluded.

By January 1891 Murphy had recovered enough to host a party for newly-married jockey Anthony Hamilton. The "Black Demon," as the press nicknamed him, had come up under trainer William Lakeland, the only white rider in the 1875 Derby.

Kingman's Derby win the following May was a personal triumph for Murphy, but it was a far cry from Murphy's 1884 victory on Buchanan when the thoroughly vicious animal he was forced to ride won by a length in a field of nine horses. Buchanan was a champion two-year-old, but when he bolted with Murphy at the Nashville track, Murphy formally rejected the contract to ride him in the Derby. Buchanan's owners held him to his contract, meaning Murphy couldn't accept another mount in the race. Black trainer William Bird — Richard Ten Broeck's trainer in the 1850s — fitted Buchanan with blinkers and he won both the Derby and Clark Stakes with Murphy in the irons.

Colonel Clark barely managed to scrape together a three-horse Derby field for 1892. In 1893, Murphy rode his last Derby mount, finishing fifth in a field of six. Murphy started training horses at the Lexington Association track, but he wasn't able to make the transition from jockey to trainer, the way Ansel, Walker and Brown had. By the end of 1895, Murphy had three Kentucky Derbys, four American Derbys, five Latonia Derbys to his credit and a 44% overall win record that has never been equalled, with the bank account to prove it. He remains the only rider to win the Derby, Oaks and Clark Handicap in a single Churchill Downs meet. There were no more reports of "champagne finishes," because, by then, Murphy was probably "flipping" to control his weight.

He died less than 24 hours after he developed pneumonia, more than likely the result of a massive lung infection. Murphy left a considerable fortune to Lucy, but she is said to have died in poverty and been buried in a potter's field, a story that has never been verified. In 1955, Isaac Murphy was the first jockey named to the newly-created Racing Hall of Fame at the National Racing Museum in Saratoga.

Years after Murphy's death, his friends marked his grave with the concrete obelisk. They made two. The other one stands on the Perkins family plot, marking the grave of James "Soup" (his favorite food) Perkins, who won wire-to-wire on Halma in the 1895 Derby, two months after he turned 15. By then, Perkins was the best-paid teenager in the country. He had won his first race at Latonia the summer he was 11. In November 1893, he signed a $4000 contract to ride with the Fleischmann Stables.

"This is a pretty soft birth for a 13-year-old colored boy," a *Thoroughbred Times* writer, who had probably never ridden anything faster than a plow horse, concluded. On the next page there was another note: "Jockey "Soup" Perkins who rode with so much success at the meeting here [Lexington], got a hard fall at Nashville last Tuesday, his mount Merry Eyes going down with him. Perkins was badly stunned and was unconscious for several hours, but the physician who attended him says that he is not injured internally. This is the first fall that Perkins ever got, as far as recalled now, and it may have the effect of making him timid and courage is Perkins' great forte."

That didn't happen. Perkins headed the list of leading American riders in 1895 with 192 victories. In May, 1911, *The Courier-Journal* noted that Perkins had just purchased a young colt and had him in training at the Downs. Three months later, Perkins died of heart disease at a race meet at Hamilton, Ontario. He was 31 and possibly, like Murphy, had destroyed his system trying to control his weight. "He can ride as light as 88 pounds," *The Thoroughbred Record* told horsemen in 1894, an indication even then that Perkins was probably flipping when it was necessary to make weight on a young horse.

Shortly after Perkins' death, friends of Perkins and Murphy placed the concrete markers in Number Two African Cemetery.

Soup's brother, trainer Will Perkins, was 54 when he died of blood poisoning from a minor foot wound. Will Perkins began his career as a jockey but his forte was training, not riding. He was an early member of the "Churchill Downs Thirty Club," limited to trainers who saddled at least one winner at 30 race meets at the Louisville track. He headed the list of successful American trainers in 1921 with 82 winners. One of his colts won the Latonia Derby in 1922, his John Finn ran third in the 1922 Kentucky Derby and his Son of John ran third in the turbulent 1925 Derby. He died the following year and his stable at the Lexington Association Track was turned over to "Rolly" Colston. Perkins was survived by his brother Edward, his stable agent, who was last interviewed by a racing reporter in the late 1980s. Ed Perkins was then in his 90s.

Raleigh "Rolly" Colston trained his first Kentucky Derby winner, Leonatus, in 1883. At the time of "Soup" Perkins' death, people still remembered that Colston's colt, ran third in the 1911 Derby, badly ridden by Jess "Long Shot" Conley, a Black jockey everybody agreed was simply not up to the job. Colston himself had ridden in the 1875 and 1876 Derbys and is another of those famous trainers who was frequently interviewed by national racing newspapers. He died in a Lexington hospital on Derby Day, May 19, 1928.

On the whole, Black trainers at the Kentucky Association track were extremely successful, in spite of an Association rule clearly stating no Negro was allowed to enter a horse in a race!

The years from 1890 to 1895 were the last good ones for African American jockeys. Their comings and goings were always noted in *The Spirit of the Times*, a New York sporting weekly.

New Orleans — March 22, 1890: "Jockey Barnes left California a couple of days ago and is expected here by Tuesday next. He comes by permission of Mr. Baldwin. He will join his own stable where it first commences operations, at St. Louis or Chicago. In the meantime he will have some of the choicest mounts along the line. He will, I think, be the king bee of jockeys on the Western (the term referred to any track west of Maryland) circuit."

"Jockey Ray did some remarkably good work in the saddle during the week, better than any other jockey here. A couple of times he was substituted for other jockeys, where suspicion was aroused, and he won both times."

". . . colored riders have made themselves felt in recent years. Murphy, Barnes and Hamilton rank with the very best and it is at least possible that Ray, in time, will be as able as the three named. There are other colored riders, such as Anderson, Stoval and Fox that are both competent and successful. In addition to all this, to their credit be it said, in the colored ranks are to be found jockeys of the most sterling honesty and integrity, and it is unfortunate that the same cannot be said of all white jockeys. In saying all this, I am not pandering to race or prejudice, but simply stating facts, albeit when I find thorough ability combined with thorough honesty I feel like going out of my way to say something in the complimentary line, and this without regard to race, color or previous condition of servitude."

These editorial comments were made the same year Klan murders reached a new peak in the South and Jim Crow laws restricting the movement of Blacks were either in place or in the works.

Kentuckian Harry "Chippie" Ray won the Kentucky Oaks in 1892 and was fourth in the 1894 Derby. Ray, who faded from the scene, was a contemporary of Alonzo Clayton who hailed from Little Rock, Arkansas.

"Lonnie" followed his brother Al to Chicago in 1888 and began riding when he was 11. He rode his first winner in 1890 at a Clifton, N. J., track, then the 90-pound jockey rode Bashford Manor Stables' homebred, Azra, to his 1892 Derby victory. Clayton, barely 15 at the time, carried 32 pounds dead-weight to make the 122 pounds required for the race. Next, he went East where *The New York World* reported Clayton was "cutting a wide swath at Saratoga and had more engagements than he could attend to."

In June, 1890, a *Spirit of the Times* reporter, then at Latonia, noted: "At Lexington recently, Isaac Murphy received a dispatch asking him to go East and join the Haggin stable. That establishment will have a strong riding team in Murphy and Ray. Both of the jockeys named are colored and that fact reminds me that nearly every prominent jockey in the West is of the colored persuasion. The East has already gobbled so many of the crack Western jockeys that there is a dearth of real good jockeys out this way, and those that have earned and attained most prominence are colored, some of them like Overton, Hollis and Britton being very black and some of them like Steppe, Williams and Allen being bright mulattoes."

Five years later, *The Times* writer, then at the February meet in New Orleans, reported to his national readership: "There is a quartet of noted colored jockeys here now in Barnes, Overton, Britton and Williams. I am sorry to state that a quartet of noted and skillful white jockeys is lacking."

Shelby "Pike" Barnes was so small he looked like an eight-year-old in the Currier & Ives print where he was pictured as one of 1888's top riders. Barnes lost the 1889 Derby on Proctor Knott, a race that broke Kentuckians' hearts and pocketbooks, but finished the season by winning the Brooklyn Derby and the Belmont Stakes. He was leading rider at Churchill Downs in 1887, 1888 and 1889.

A new face from Georgia, Willie Simms, born in 1880, headed the American list of winning riders in 1894 with 228 victories to his credit. Simms won the Kentucky and Latonia Derbys on Ben Brush in 1896 and the Kentucky Derby on Plaudit in 1898. In 1894 he was the summer's "invincible hero" of New York's Jerome Park before leaving for England, where he was deemed a failure because he rode high in the saddle — a position the English detested.

"Monkeyship has supplanted jockeyship," aristocratic turfites complained. Simms returned to America where wealthy New York horse owners stood in line for his services. Simms' 1895 income was reported to be $20,000, two years after a New York stock market crash left many wage-earners jobless and on the streets.

When a second American rider, Indiana's Tod Sloan, went to England, and rode Simms' style in an even more exaggerated "monkey on a stick" fashion and won, English jockeys copied him. The Simms-Sloan technique eventually brought to an end the long-legged, spurring riding style that cut Thoroughbreds' sides wide open during races.

After Simms got too big to ride — he was last interviewed at the Downs shortly after the 1909 Derby where he told a reporter he would ride again if he could make the weight — he trained steeplechasers, a sport in which his riding style was a distinct advantage. Simms died at age 47 in Asbury Park, N. J. The list of Simms' stakes wins, including the Belmont, extended his obituary by half a page. He was the second, and last, Black rider inducted into the Racing Hall of Fame, 22 years after Murphy.

In 1897, the country suffered a second, even more severe, economic depression, brought on by Wall Street stock manipulators. Within two years, all but a handful of the biggest racing stables in the East and California were forced into bankruptcy. The golden days were over for everybody. Historian Lyman Weeks published his book on New York racing just before the depression hit. One out of every seven jockeys pictured in Weeks' book were African Americans, as were 20 trainers. "That Lexington, Kentucky should produce a proportionately larger number of distinguished horsemen than any other place in the United States, has long been a foregone conclusion," Weeks wrote. The men, but for Weeks' book, long since forgotten, survived hard times by finding work wherever they could.

In 1894, New York sanctioned a group of wealthy businessmen, organized as The Jockey Club, to act as a regulatory agency for racing, empowered to issue licenses or rule men off tracks. From Weeks' book, we know they did not discriminate against Blacks before 1897. Since a number of Blacks became steeplechase jockeys and trainers, it appears that, in New York at least, the reason for the disappearance Black riders was the double knockout punch of the 1897 Depression and anti-gambling legislation.

The last Kentucky-born Black jockey to make an international name for himself was Jimmy Winkfield. One of a family of 17 born in a two-room shack in Cadentown near Lexington, the 15-year-old burst on the scene in 1898, causing a four-horse pileup in his first race that immediately earned him a year's suspension. When he returned to riding, he quickly gained the reputation of being "a gentleman on the ground and a demon in the saddle." In 1901 Winkfield rode 161 winners, including victories in the Kentucky, New Orleans, Memphis and Latonia Derbys. He returned to Louisville to win a second Kentucky Derby in 1902 and ride in the 1903 race. By 1904, Winkfield was riding in Russia. He later claimed weight problems caused him to leave America, but it was rumored that Winkfield had double-crossed John E. Madden and Madden had threatened his career, if not his life. Horsemen got Winkfield out of the country in no time flat!

That put Winkfield in the vanguard of jockeys forced to follow owners and Thoroughbreds to Europe when the New York Legislature closed New York tracks in 1910. He was a star in Russia before the 1917 Revolution forced him to flee again. He settled in Paris, France, rode until he was 47, and then became a successful trainer. When the Germans invaded, Winkfield was able to escape through Portugal to bring his family safely to America. After living abroad, he found the racism in this country unbearable. He returned to France after the war and, except for returning to the Kentucky Derby in 1961, when he was almost barred from the Brown Hotel press party at which he was guest of honor, he lived abroad for the rest of his life.

In August 1900, *The Thoroughbred Record* contained an ominous warning under the heading "JOCKEY WAR AT CHICAGO." A race war, instigated by white riders, resulted in rough riding, fines and suspensions. Covington newspapers had reported similar problems with white riders attacking successful Black riders at Latonia the year before.

Yet, Black jockey Jimmie Lee made the racing world sit up and take notice in 1907 when he rode six winners in the seven-race card at Churchill Downs. "Taking into consideration the prices laid against his mounts" *The Thoroughbred Record* commented, "it is one of the most remarkable performances ever achieved on any race course." Lee won the 1907 Kentucky Oaks and had mounts in the 1907, 1908 and 1909 Kentucky Derbys. Weeks after a "bad looking fall" at the Downs, Lee repeated his six-win day at Latonia in 1908, then was on five winners twice in one week at New Orleans. Lee went to California, where he was not successful, then returned to Kentucky where his career went steadily downhill. He died at Derby time in 1915 at his Raceland, La., home. According to his obituary, Lee died penniless, although he had earned a small fortune during his lifetime.

After 1905, the ranks of Black riders began to thin out as segregation and Klan atrocities in Kentucky and the South increased. Except for noting the success of jockey Clarence "Pick" Dishman, member of a farflung Bluegrass horse family that included trainer Oscar Dishman Jr., *The Thoroughbred Record* contented itself with publishing reminiscences and obituaries of well-known Black horsemen.

Babe Hurd, 1882 Kentucky Derby winner, later a successful steeplechase jockey, died in 1928 at Longridge Farm on Paris Pike. Derby jockey Alfred "Monk" Overton died in Cincinnati in 1935. He had been a successful trainer for many years. No record has been found for Erskine "Babe" Henderson between the time he rode Joe Cotton to three 1885 derby victories — the Kentucky, the Tennessee and the Coney Island — and the 1913 Kentucky Derby when *The Courier-Journal* reported the 49-year-old Henderson was back at the Downs as a trainer still small enough to gallop his own horses. Even less is known about four-time Derby rider Isaac Lewis, who won on Montrose in 1887, except for the listing of his numerous stakes victories in the late '80s and early 1890s.

Thomas Britton, three times leading rider at Churchill Downs in the early 1890s, died after a fall at Washington Park. Ed West died at Saratoga. Tommy Knight was killed by a train en route to Matt Winn's Juarez track. Isaac Murphy's friend, Anthony Hamilton, eventually went to Europe and died of tuberculosis in his private railroad car in Germany, "swathed in sable with diamond rings glittering on every finger," his obituary noted.

Once racing got back on an even keel following World War I, there were far more Black trainers in the business than are reflected by Derby entries. When Lexington native Marshall Lilly died at age 90 he was best known as the Whitney family's assistant trainer. As James Rowe Sr.'s exercise rider he conditioned unbeaten Colin and Kentucky Derby winner Regret, as well as training Derby entrant, Sgt. Byrne, in 1934.

Louisvillian Jake Bachelor worked the night shift at International Harvester, then went to the Downs to train his horses. "The racetrack is something that once you get in it, it never gets out," he explained when he won the Debutante Stakes in 1972.

Arthur "Tats" Perrosier celebrated his 100th birthday in 1992. He was J. Graham Brown's advisor for 30 years but his name does not appear in the records as Brown's trainer. Such was Brown's peculiar brand of racism that he privately supported African American charities and educational institutions, but would not allow Blacks access to his hotel except by the back door.

Louisvillian Carl Sitgraves first rode steeplechasers and made a name for himself as a successful Thoroughbred trainer long before Brown asked him to come to the Brown Hotel and discuss taking on the Brown Hotel stables. When Sitgraves was told colored people were required to use the freight elevator, he turned on his heel and left. Sitgraves and his wife, Essie, who raced her own stable of Thoroughbreds in the 1960s, live within walking distance of the Downs. Time has diminished neither Sitgraves' stature nor his dignity.

One of the Sitgraves' neighbors was Chuck Walker, a man John E. Madden's biographer references only as Madden's stable foreman. A white sports announcer who grew up at Hamburg Place remembered Chuck Walker well. According to him, Madden required unquestioning obedience from his employees, with the following disclaimer: "Do as I tell you in all things, unless Walker tells you different, then do as he says." Walker broke yearlings for Madden and supervised the shoeing of Madden's two-year-olds. After Madden's death, Walker, who received a pension from Madden's estate, moved to Louisville and worked as a clocker at Churchill Downs.

The most recent obituary for a Black jockey was written Dec. 12, 1994, when 54-year-old Baltimore native, Jimmy Thornton, died at the Charles Town, W. V., track. He had ridden steeplechasers for Hall of Famers Mike and Paddy Smithwick, then switched to flat racing and won his first race at Bowie Race Course in 1962. In 1993, he beat Pat Day in a photo finish on Preakness Day at Pimlico. After his death, trainers recalled Thornton's ability to get along with any horse. "Just a natural-born horseman," they said. "Always a gentleman," Mike Smithwick ended — the highest accolade a Southerner can receive.

Public and media attention is usually focused on the stars at the racetrack. Only people within the industry understand how much depends on men who work on the Thoroughbred farms. PASSING OF VENERABLE HORSEMAN read the headlines above Henry Overton's obituary on Sept. 18, 1926. Robert A. Alexander bought

Overton in Tennessee when the boy was 10. He was trained to be Alexander's personal servant and might have remained so had Alexander not bought the stallion Lexington in 1855.

After Alexander purchased Ansel, Ansel trained Overton — first as a jockey, then as Woodburn's stud groom. In that capacity, Overton stayed at Woodburn until Alexander's death in 1867, then went to work for Senator Johnson N. Camden's Hartland Stud. There was never a day when Overton didn't ride, until health problems forced him to retire. The last foal crop Overton supervised went to the Kentucky Association track the week before he died in 1926. Overton's passing, *The Thoroughbred Record* observed, "marks another break in the fragile chain linking the older generation of horsemen with those of the present day."

This was the same decade that saw Will Harbut rise to international fame as Man o' War's groom. Harbut was a horseman, a showman and more. For 17 years he ruled the great champion's schedule with an iron hand that protected the stallion from celebrities who considered themselves more important than Harbut's pride and joy. They were the most-photographed team in the country. Newspapers printed accounts of Harbut's shooing visiting dignitaries from the barn when it was time for "Big Red" to nap, but at birthday celebrations for the horse, Harbut ate at a table by himself. After a stroke forced Harbut to retire in 1946, Man o' War went into a depression from which he never recovered. Man and horse died within months of each other in 1947. Harbut's obituary appeared front and center on *The New York Times* obituary page, over that of a nuclear scientist. Harbut's son Tom followed in his father's footsteps as a stud groom, breeding and owning 1962 Kentucky Derby runner Touch Bar.

Sam Ransom broke Triple Crown winner Count Fleet for taxifleet owner for John D. Hertz, advising Hertz early on not to sell the promising colt to Claiborne Farms' A. B. "Bull" Hancock. Ransom eventually worked for Claiborne and went to A. B. Hancock III's Stone Farm "just for the day" to help with foaling in 1973, shortly after Claiborne management responsibilities were assigned to Hancock's younger brother Seth. Ransom became Stone Farm's first employee and, before his death in 1990, saw Stone Farm produce two Derby winners, Gato Del Sol and Sunday Silence.

Clem Brooks was Spendthrift Farm's answer to Will Harbut. He and the $1-million horse, Nashua, were one of Lexington's biggest tourist attraction in the 1960s. Brooks told a story that demonstrates the relationship between a farm owner and his stud groom as well as any. There wasn't a horse Brooks couldn't handle, but he couldn't abide snakes. When Combs' son threw a garden snake at Brooks, Brooks spanked him. Mrs. Combs demanded that her husband fire Brooks, who made no apology for the action he had taken. Leslie Combs debated briefly between upholding his son's position and losing the man who handled tourists and Nashua with equal ease. Brooks stayed at the farm until it closed.

There is an art to managing Thoroughbreds in the sales ring, especially at Keeneland, where the Thoroughbred world converges every July. Thomas "Buck" Evans was the dean of the Keeneland yearling handlers. As a child he would cut school and jump on John Madden's polo ponies in the field. Evans' mentor, trainer C. E. Greene, taught him how to break yearlings, hence the name "Buck." Evans conditioned horses until his death in 1989, but it in the Keeneland Sales ring that he achieved lasting fame. Francis "Frank" Wilson is the man who led Warner Jones' $13,100,000 Seattle Dancer through the auction in 1985. He has been with Jonabell Farm since 1949, is a deacon in the Baptist Church and sold a stakes-winning filly of his own at Keeneland in 1979.

In 1952, sportswriter Prescott Sullivan told it like it was. "Officially, horse racing does not discriminate but it has long permitted a Jim Crow conspiracy to stand. [Unlike baseball] racing's color line is of more recent origin. It goes back about forty years. Prior to that time there were many colored riders and some of them were rated among the best in the business." The nature and legacy of that "best" is only now being recognized.

William Tregonwell Frampton

Chapter Eleven

Farriers, Vets and Trainers

The farriers' craft is among the oldest known to mankind, but veterinary science, once considered a part of horseshoeing, did not exist as a separate profession until the 19th Century. So many problems begin with horses' feet that, regardless of talent or appearance, their feet make or break them. An inept farrier can "nail a horse to the ground;" a good one can give him wings.

Farriery, the art of shoeing horses, has always been a well-paid profession, one that has not changed much in a thousand years. All the breeding and training in the world means nothing if a horse is crippled by bad shoeing. The average horse must have his feet trimmed and his shoes reset or replaced every six weeks. Farriery is dangerous, backbreaking, highly-skilled labor which will never be supplanted by machines or computers. To any horse owner, a good farrier is worth his weight in gold.

Freeman Rolly Blue announced the opening of his center-city blacksmith's shop in the April 1818 *Kentucky Gazette*. It was on Water Street, "near the residence of Dr. Campbell and opposite the Upper [Street] Market House" — the 19th Century equivalent of being located between a medical center and a shopping mall! Blue did both iron work and farriery and his life can be traced through the records of his shop.

Young men apprenticed themselves to farriers by choice — the attraction seems to be divinely ordained by a combination of skill, determination, patience, a love of horses and a strong back. The typical apprenticeship began when the boy was around 10 and lasted 10 years. Old time farriery in Kentucky was a working brotherhood that came close to being color-blind — until newcomers who didn't understand what the work entailed got into hobby racing in the 1920s and brought their prejudices to the Bluegrass with them.

Farm farriers who worked with young stock were particularly vulnerable. Two of the most famous, William "Jelly" Caulder and John Madison, remembered being fired by new management during the Depression because they charged $1 to trim yearlings' feet. "A white man," they were told, "can do it for 50 cents." Six months later, when most of the farm's yearlings were either crooked or crippled, they were asked to return. Caulder and Madison put the farm back on their list, charging $2 a head, and, as they related the story, "Nobody ever questioned another bill!"

The legacy of the African American farrier stretched the length and width of the Bluegrass. George Tompkins, who early on experimented with treating horses' feet with magnetized metal, trained not only his son, Ralph, and a grandson, Barrie Tompkins, but white farrier McNair Kerswill and Black farrier, Jackie Thompson, both of whom shod more than one Kentucky Derby winner.

The legendary Andy Merritt, denied a licence in Illinois because of his race, came to Kentucky and specialized in racetrack farriery. Merritt had quite a repetoire of tunes he played with his hammer and anvil while he was made shoes. He was working at the Detroit Race Course when he died in 1990. His son, David Merritt, is a farrier in Florida today.

Oldtimers remember when a 1950s-era statewide farriers' meeting was almost called off because of the then-prevailing patterns of segregation in Louisville. When the Seelbach Hotel announced its intention not to seat the groups' Black members, the groups' president left his hospital bed to inform the Seelbach that his organization would either eat together or they wouldn't eat at the Seelbach. For one evening, the Seelbach was an integrated hotel.

Until 1994, the oldest working farrier in Kentucky was Danville's Roy Neal. Neal apprenticed under a German farrier and could shoe Thoroughbreds, Standardbreds, Saddlebreds and Walking Horses with equal ease. The brilliant Saddlebred stallion, Wing Commander, was Neal's pride and joy. Neal continued to "nail on a few every day," until he was incapacitated by a light stroke in August, 1994, his 80th summer. Like Caulder and Madison, Neal, the senior Tompkins, Thompson, Merritt and Kerswill are all members of the Farrier's International Hall of Fame.

Good, old-fashioned horse doctors — sometimes medical doctors who specialized in animal care — did a little bit of everything, treating all the livestock on a farm or plantation. Although there were classes in veterinary medicine in Italy as early as the 1600s, Americans usually earned their "doc"torates by apprenticing under other veterinarians, in much the same way farriers learned their skills. There was no separate organization for those who specialized in equine medicine until 1954, but by the 1850s there were any number of books available on horse anatomy and home remedies. Since horses can't explain where they hurt, the skill was, and still is today, in quickly and accurately diagnosing what is wrong. Horses have one-way systems — they cannot regurgitate food — so they can kill themselves by "eating like a horse" unless they get help fast. Horses' feet act as sensors for their entire system. Today the highly complex blood flow in horses' limbs is just beginning to be understood. Only recently has research been funded to study laminitis, an inflammation of the sensitive tissue of the hooves most people know only as "the disease that killed Secretariat."

History and pedigree, jockeys, juleps and burgoo — everything in Thoroughbred racing can be explained, with one exception — trainers. Trainers defy explanation and categorization. They're just born to be trainers and that's it. William Tregonwell Frampton was the first English trainer of note. He deserves mention in any racing book because he held on to his job as Keeper of the Running Horse through the reigns of four British monarchs. William III gave him an allowance for "the Maintenance of 10 boys, their lodgings, &c., and for provisions of Hay, Oats, Bread, and all other necessaries for 10 race horses," along with a salary of a thousand pounds a year. Frampton was a known woman hater, passionately fond of horse racing, cock fights and gambling. He never changed the style of his clothing and was frequently seen at court, where, regardless of his uncouth appearance, he was well received. Queen Anne called him Governor Frampton. He was almost 90 when he died.

Up until the 20th Century, most trainers came from the ranks of jockeys, having learned their skills from grooming, riding and conditioning horses. One of the secrets of being a successful trainer, besides the ability to get along with horses and the people who work with horses, in having the knack for talking without saying anything and sounding as if you sincerely mean every word of it.

John E. Madden's admirers called him a hard, shrewd, self-confident man, unemotional, suspicious and a loner, but "no horse of his ever met a surprised Madden in the winner's circle" to quote Kent Hollingsworth, his biographer. Madden could use the English language to confuse a bettor to the point where the individual simply gave up.

"John E. Madden certainly is a very peculiar man," one disgruntled turfman complained. "Before the first race today I asked him what he thought of his horse's chances. Well, you should have heard the scientific way he diagnosed the race, setting forth how his horse might win, and then again how it was possible for him to lose. I was just looking for a tip, but when Madden got through talking I went and sat down and didn't go near the betting ring. And that horse came home with better than 10-1 against him!"

Low odds do not a wealthy trainer make.

Trainers must be smart enough to retain clients while appearing not to know what their horses are capable of doing. Those who do not use language to obfuscate, resort to a silence that makes "Silent Cal" Coolidge seem like a chatterbox in comparison. The best example of this I ever encountered on the backside of Churchill Downs was the trainer, then unknown to me, who always came into the track kitchen with a sad look on his face.

"How're your horses doing?" he was asked one morning when his mood seemed especially bleak. He shook his head sadly. "If my horses can run they sure ain't told me about it," he replied.

I inquired about the man — suicide is not unheard of in the racing business. "That's W——— B———," I was told, "he's won three stakes since the beginning of the meet."

No trainer ever committed suicide, so the saying goes, with a two-year-old in his barn!

Chapter Twelve

Kaintuckie "Talk"

You can't get there from here if you don't know how to pronounce where you are or where you're going. Kentucky shares with
the rest of the South an irrationally idiosyncratic approach to the
English language. Even within the borders of the state — indeed
within adjoining neighborhoods in a county as large as Jefferson —
the natives don't always understand each other. From 1780 to 1912
the state split itself into 120 counties, which says something about
how long-standing some neighborly misunderstandings have been.

Kentuckians also take a certain pride in confusing visitors,
leading to some wonderful stories like the one about the two men
who were passing through Woodford County, on their way to
Keeneland, discussing how to pronounce the name of Woodford's
county seat, Versailles. The first man said: "The city was named to
honor King Louis XVI. It's pronounced Vair-sigh, just like Louis'
palace in France."

His friend disagreed. "It's pronounced Ver-sales," he insisted.
They decided to pull into a fast food emporium, order lunch and
settle their dispute at the drive-thru window. So, after counting his
change, the driver asked the cashier, "Could you please tell me —
real slow — where we are?" The woman was more than happy to
oblige. "Bur-ger King," she replied.

Actually, pronouncing Versailles correctly is a lot harder than
either of them knew. The V has just a hint of F to it, so it comes close
to, but is not really, pronounced Fer-sales. If you can't handle that,
stick to Ver-sales, but never Vair-sigh!

Versailles is just up the road from Keeneland, where this
"true story" happened. Shortly after King's Island, a Cincinnati-area
amusement park opened, a Keeneland meet opened as well. State
troopers were at the gates directing traffic when a station wagon
with out-of-state plates, full of children, stopped by one of the troopers. The thoroughly-confused driver rolled down his window and
asked, "Is this Keene's Island?" He had obviously gotten directions
from a Kentuckian to get there!

Paris, Ky., is on the other side of Lexington in Bourbon
County. "Paris" may look like a two-syllable word, but you'll be

better off pronouncing it "pairs" or "pares," never "paree" so it doesn't sound uppity, or, worse yet, foreign. Like Versailles, Bourbon County was to honor Louis XVI, Bourbon being his family name. Bourbon, the distinctive whiskey, a fermented mixture of homegrown corn and the local limestone spring water, took its name from the area where it was first produced and not vice versa.

When M. Lewis Clark visited France in the 1870s, he brought back a wagering machine called the pari-mutuel, from the words "pari" meaning a bet or wager, and "mutuel," a mutual benefit association. Machine betting was in its infancy. The most popular method of betting in France at that time was with "le tout" — the bookmaker. As in England and America, they were corrupters of the sport, so much so that by 1887 the French government, outraged by race-fixing, instructed the police that bookmakers were to be removed from all tracks, which created as many problems as it solved. The French government mulled things over for four years. In 1891 they approved track-operated pari-mutuel wagering. "Pari" — a bet — had nothing to do with Paris, the city; but turf writers called the machines "Paris-mutuels" because it sounded more highfalutin, and the name stuck. It's purely a coincidence that Paris-mutuels hit their stride at the same time some of the best-known Thoroughbred farms in the world were being developed around Paris and Versailles, Ky! However you choose to pronounce them, Paris and Versailles are not to be missed. They abound with good, small restaurants and interesting shops — another reason not to take serious pronunciation questions to Burger King.

The city of Louisville was also named to honor King Louis XVI, who lost his head in the French Revolution shortly thereafter. In the beginning, natives, regardless of what part of the city they lived in, pronounced it "Lou-e-ville" and everybody got along just fine. At least we all knew where we were. Then, about 25 years ago, Lou-e-ville's movers and shakers decided the place needed a new image, something more upscale than Lou-e-villians could produce. They hired consultants, from out of town, of course, to give us a new image. LOuisVillE, they pointed out, spells LOVE, so "We Love Louisville" became their campaign cry. Then they searched for something more creative — like saying Louisville after quickly swallowing two mint juleps in the infield on a really warm Derby afternoon. Lou-e-ville became "Luellville" and the battle between real Lou-e-villians and Luellville wannabees has raged ever since. Several years ago, The Louisville and Jefferson County Convention and Visitors Bureau, a cheery group of individuals who want people to visit the city regardless of the way they pronounce it, decided to resolve the conflict. Emblazoned on banners and t-shirts are the words: Looavull. Luhvul. Lewisville. Looaville. Looeyville. Louisville! YOUR KIND OF PLACE. . . ANY WAY YOU SAY IT.

The climate may explain why many native Louisvillians sound the way they do. There is ample evidence to suggest that early pioneers, land hungry though they were, were way too smart to settle along the banks of the Ohio. The site was little more than a network of mosquito infested stagnant ponds. General George Rogers Clark, founder of the city, came here with troops in 1778 and brought civilians along as a cover, not wishing to give away his plan to invade the Old Northwest Territory. If a few of the hardy pioneers hadn't put down roots and refused to leave, there'd be no one here, even today. The problem is the humidity, which encourages ragweed and pollen growth. Louisville natives speak softly, as if they had gills. It is not an unpleasant sound, but important communications, especially directions, should always be checked for accuracy.

If you travel out the Bardstown Road along 31W you will eventually end up in the city of the same name — the hospitality, burgoo and bourbon capital of Nelson County. For reasons I cannot explain, but attribute to an unending case of post-nasal congestion, all native Louisvillians refer to the city as "Bargetown." As it was named for David Baird, one of the original owners of the hundred acres set aside for settlement, it should be, and indeed started out being, Bairdstown. Have lunch at any of the charming restaurants near the courthouse or drive around the old neighborhoods and look at the architecture and you'll fall in love with the place, even if, when you get back, you can't say for certain where you've been.

There was once a racetrack on the Shelbyville Road, near where Middletown is today. Histories indicate that a stagecoach traveled regularly between Shelbyville in Shelby County and Louisville, when the races were in session. Named for Isaac Shelby, first and fifth governor of Kentucky, the name should be foolproof. Of course, it isn't. Pronounce it Shel-be-ville and everyone will know you're new to town. "Shebbyville, gently slurred as you say it, is the way to go.

Short of taking a course in linguistics from a native before you set foot in horse country, there is no sure fire way to talk Kentucky, but there are guidelines. Be creative, take your time, speak softly and pretend you have a mouth full of grits. Always smile and never be afraid to pull out a map and point to where you want to go. It may be the only way to get here from there!

Chapter Thirteen

Authentic Kentucky Recipes

If they ever outlaw cholesterol, Kentucky will have to secede from the Union. Somehow good food, REAL FOOD, and Thoroughbred racing just go together. "Low-fat racing fare" is a contradiction in terms. On a beautiful spring morning, the appetite demands country pleasures — eggs and grits, country ham and beaten biscuits. A nippy fall afternoon at Keeneland without burgoo would be an act of deprivation. When it comes to food, life is too short for anything but the best. Moderate, if you must, how much you eat at a backside kitchen breakfast or a Derby brunch, but don't deny yourself the experience of these classic feasts.

Kentuckians have wonderfully strange names for what we cook, so learning the history of a dish is as much of an adventure as learning how to prepare it. Years ago I assembled all the ingredients for biscuits and told my daughter we were going to make them "starting from scratch." She checked the flour, salt, lard and water laid out on the table, and asked "where's the scratch?"

The term harks back to colonial times when two gentlemen wanted to test their horses' speed in an informal match race, away from public viewing. They picked a clear, straight stretch of road and drew a line in the dirt with a stick. The race began at that point, hence "starting from scratch."

BEATEN BISCUITS

The rest of the world bakes biscuits, Kentuckians beat them first. If you buy a commercial product labeled "beaten biscuits" they will, in all probability, taste like paste, and since country ham, if not top quality, tends to be dry and stringy, the result can be akin to chewing salty cardboard. The true beaten biscuit melts in your mouth, begging for butter or a clear jelly. For a real recipe — one that does not use equipment to discipline the dough — try this one from Cissy Gregg's cookbook, published by *The Courier-Journal* in the 1950s.

7 cups flour	2 to 4 teaspoons sugar
1 teaspoon baking powder	1 cup lard
1 teaspoon salt	1 1/3 cup whole milk

Sift the flour and measure. Then sift flour, baking powder,

salt and sugar together three times. Cut in the lard, using the finger tips or two knives, until these ingredients are of a finer consistency that when mixed for ordinary biscuits but not quite as fine as for pastry. Add the cold milk to make a stiff dough. The dough is beaten by hand — you can use a flat iron or a heavy spoon. Beat the dough out until it is 1/4" thick, fold and beat again. Repeat this until the dough is smooth, glossy and has blisters. It takes about 30 minutes of beating to aerate the dough — or use the "200 beats for home-folks and 500 beats for company" rule. Finally, roll the dough out to the 1/4" thickness and cut with a small biscuit cutter. A 2" cutter is too big, improvise with a small glass if necessary.

All beaten biscuits must have their tops pricked with a fork. Whether you have a three or four row pattern is up to you, but be sure the fork goes clear through the biscuit and hits the pan. The beating and folding has created thin layers of dough so the biscuits will yawn as they bake. Bake at 350 degrees for 20 to 25 minutes. The full recipe makes 6 to 7 dozen biscuits; you might start with half the recipe if your arm is not up to par.

•Flour is flour until you've been to the Weisenberger Mill, on the banks of the South Elkhorn Creek near Midway, Kentucky. Run by fifth-generation descendants of German immigrant Augustus Weisenberger, the mill grinds 7,500 pounds of Kentucky-grown wheat and corn daily, smooth as silk, fine as talcum powder. This is a site to visit when Keeneland is in session, spring or fall. Drop by and they'll sell you a 5-pound bag of flour for under $1.50. They ship a variety of flours — and Alabama-ground, Adams Old Fashioned Whole Heart Grits. Write or call Weisenberger Flour Mills, Box 215, Midway, KY 40347, (606) 254-5282. If you live any distance away, the shipping will cost more than the flour and be well worth it!

COUNTRY HAM

The British are responsible not only for the pedigree of the Thoroughbred horse, they have developed more breeds of livestock than any nation on earth. Lexingtonians, Senator Henry Clay among them, were among the first to import fancy breeds of cattle, hogs, chickens and sheep from England and Scotland. Farmers brought their prized specimens to Bluegrass county fairs where ribbons and elegantly engraved silver beakers, called "julep cups," were awarded as trophies. Because corn was abundant, beef and pork, along with bourbon, were among the state's first cash crops.

In the old days, farmers turned their cattle out into fields of standing corn at the end of summer to fatten them up for the long trek to market. Cows trampled as much as they ate. Hogs, being scavengers, made the waste profitable, eating whatever the cows left behind, before following them to market.

The fall hog slaughter provided a family with pork, bacon and hams that were salted and hung from the rafters of the smokehouse to slow cure over an open fire, a process that hardened the thick skin, protecting the succulent center. From pig to table the process took a year or longer. Salt was an expensive commodity on the frontier, so country ham was a luxury. It still is!

The older the ham, the moldier the outside becomes. This story may sound like a tall tale, but variations of it are told by too many remorseful natives not to be true. Kentuckians who had visited friends above the Mason-Dixon line wanted to thank their hosts in as grand a manner as possible and sent them a whole country ham. For months, there was no word of acknowledgment for the expensive gift. Finally they inquired.

"Oh," came the embarrassed reply, "we didn't know how to tell you, but the ham you sent us was all moldy, so we threw it out."

Anyone who sends a real country ham without instructions should not hold the recipient accountable for where it ends up. Only instructions, like these from Mrs. Carl Fischer, Jr., will render it a delicacy.

Scrub the ham with a stiff brush to clean it and remove any mold. Cover the ham with cold water and soak for 24 hours. (A lard can makes a good container). Discard the soak water. Again cover the ham with water and place it on the stove. Add 1 quart of vinegar, 1 cup of brown sugar, 1 sliced, unpeeled orange, a few red pepper pods, a pinch of allspice, and several whole cloves. Bring the water to the boiling point (container should be covered), then lower the heat to the lowest setting which allows the ham to steam until done. Cook 15 minutes per pound or approximately 3 1/2 hours. Remove from the heat and let the ham remain in the cooking water until the water is cool. When cool, remove the ham from the water and cut off any skin and excess fat. Leave the bone in. Score the fat and decorate it with a mixture of pineapple juice and brown sugar, dotted with cloves and cherries. Bake at 350 degrees long enough to brown the fat and the topping (about 20 minutes). An hour before serving, slice the ham very thin and allow it to reach room temperature to bring out the full flavor.

If you haven't the energy or the muscle to do more than read this recipe, buy country ham, preferably presliced. Be prepared to stand in line, especially at Derby time, and pay the going price for top quality meat. Just remember that a little country ham goes a long way. Some stores will ship ham, but not during the heat of summer. If you buy some and plan to travel with it, regardless of the season, be sure to seal the package. Country ham grease is potent stuff and the aroma lingers forever!

•Probably the best known hams in the state are those produced by Finchville Farms. Margaret Davis and her brother inherited the business their father started in his country store shortly after World War II. Finchville Farms hams are still cured with salt, red and black pepper and sugar, without nitrates or nitrites, just the way they were back in the days when a car was a luxury and a Kentucky highway was two narrow lanes of blacktop. Even then, the word got out about Finchville Farms hams and folks would risk the back roads just to buy one. The world has changed around those hams but they still age naturally, chilling in the winter and going through the June sweats (salt keeps the meat from spoiling) outside in barns. Production is limited and Margaret Davis will tell you that folks in big cities like New York do know their number. If you want to visit the store, Finchville is eight miles south of Shelbyville. Call 1-800-678-1521 for their brochure.

•In Louisville, The Cheddar Box sells Finchville Farms ham by the pound. The store, a source for other hard-to-locate Kentucky delicacies and desserts, is located at 3909 Chenoweth Square, Louisville, KY 40207. Telephone (502) 893-2324.

HENRY BAIN SAUCE

The Pendennis Club, Churchill Down's founder M. Lewis Clark, Jr.'s bachelor quarters, thrives today at Second and Muhammad Ali Boulevard, a bastion of conservative politics, old Louisville families and good cooking. Samuel Churchill is credited with naming the organization after Thackeray's personable character, "Major Pendennis," when it was founded in 1881.

African American Henry Bain went to work there as an elevator boy shortly after the club opened. At the time of his death, just weeks before the 1928 Derby, he was a legend, one of the city's most recognized individuals, a man who knew, it was said, the names and pedigrees of everyone in Louisville society. Roland Hayes, the great lyric tenor, was his nephew, and Bain arranged for him to make his professional debut at the Pendennis Club in 1910.

On May 3, 1928, *The Courier-Journal* published an editorial about Henry Bain which concluded: "Not among all the members of the Pendennis Club, nor among the thousands throughout the world who have enjoyed its hospitality, is there or has there been a truer gentleman than was Henry Bain, for 40 years in its service — most of them as its headwaiter."

"Captain Henry" was a commanding presence, with a staff of buss boys and waiters at his beck and call, by the time he created the gourmet sauce that has delighted generations of Louisvillians. He is said to have prepared the first batch in the Club's dining room, in response to a group of men who asked him to create a condiment for their steaks. Bain's sauce was an immediate hit. Meant to accompany roast beef, steak or pork, it works on an hors d'oeuvre tray when poured over softened cream cheese and served with toasted crackers.

In a very large bowl combine the following:
1 12-ounce bottle chili sauce
1 10-ounce bottle A-1 Steak Sauce
1 14-ounce bottle catsup
1 10-ounce bottle Worcestershire Sauce
1 12-ounce jar Sharwood's Major Grey Mango Chutney
Dash or more Tabasco Sauce

Mix thoroughly, pour in half-pint jars (the recipe makes about 7 jars) and refrigerate.

BENEDICTINE

Victorian Louisville provided business opportunities for women in the distaff trades. Madams, dressmakers and caterers could get rich. Jenny Benedict certainly did. Her food emporium and catering service was legendary. Benedictine made her immortal. Spread it on fresh white crustless bread for finger sandwiches, slather it on country ham or a cold turkey sandwich, stuff it in a tomato shell or dip chips in it. Then repent at your leisure. There is no reason for eating benedictine except pure enjoyment.

Peel, slice and chop a medium cucumber as fine as you can, by hand. Some people grate the cucumber or put it in a blender. **DON'T**. It makes the benedictine runny. The old recipe called for adding half a medium-sized grated onion to the cucumber, but you will find that unless you use a mild Vidalia onion, the taste can be a little bitter. Hand blend the cucumber into an 8-ounce package of softened Philadelphia Cream Cheese, colored with a drop or two of green food coloring to turn it a delicate spring green. Mix by hand until smooth. Instead of onion, here I add garlic salt to taste, killing two birds with one stone. As a concession to cholesterol, I use Philadelphia Light Cream Cheese and can't tell the difference. With any other brand, it just isn't the same.

CHEESE DOLLARS

From Midway, Ky.'s Holly Hill Inn comes a recipe with two names. In Louisville, they're cheese straws. In Lexington, they're cheese dollars. Since this is a book about racing, cheese dollars make better sense. By any name, they appear on Bluegrass buffet tables all year long.

1 pound sharp cheddar cheese, grated	1/2 cup butter
1 teaspoon salt	2 cups flour
3/4 teaspoon red pepper	
1/2 cup parmesan cheese	

In the bowl of a food processor, combine the first five room-temperature ingredients until smooth. Chill dough for 20 minutes. On a pastry board, sprinkle out 1/2 cup parmesan cheese and roll out the dough to 1/4" thickness. Cut with a cookie cutter into small rounds and bake on an ungreased baking sheet at 350 degrees for 10-12 minutes. This ends the section on finger foods. Now we get to serious eating.

CHICKEN A LA KEENE

This racing delight comes down to us as a pallid luncheon dish, "chicken a la king." Its history is nothing short of noble and, when properly prepared, it is far from pale. James R. Keene was an English-born Californian who went to New York in the 1870s to enlarge his already considerable fortune on the turf and Wall Street. He bought a yearling from Kentucky's famous Woodburn Farm and named the colt after his son, Foxhall. In 1880, Foxhall was the first American horse to win the Grand Prix in Paris, then Foxhall took England by storm, winning the prestigious Ascot Gold Cup in 1882. Keene was an enormously popular man in England, what is known as a credit to the turf. The night of his Gold Cup victory, so the story goes, he dined with princes and kings. The chef named the dish he created that evening "Chicken a la Keene." Properly prepared, it's fit for royalty!

1/3 cup butter
1/3 cup flour
1 cup chicken broth
1 1/2 cups whole milk, or preferably, cream
Salt and pepper to taste
Meat from one cooked hen, cubed
1/2 pound mushrooms
1 pimento, cut in strips
1 green pepper, cut in strips
Sherry
Pastry tart shells

Melt butter in top of double boiler; stir flour in slowly. Gradually add chicken broth and milk, stirring constantly. Season to taste. Saute mushrooms, pimento, green pepper in more butter until they are tender but not overdone. Fold them into the sauce along with the chicken and add sherry to taste. Simmer very gently to meld the flavors and serve in tart shells. For color, paprika may be sprinkled lightly on the top.

HOT BROWN

It is sad that the biography of a man who did so much, in his own unique fashion, for horse racing in Louisville should be relegated to the kitchen, but there is no other way to tell J. Graham Brown's story. Besides, were he alive, the iconoclastic entrepreneur might get a kick out of it.

Brown was born in Indiana, the son of middle class Scots-Irish parents. At the time of his death in 1969, he was worth, more or less, $100-million, profits from his Southern lumber empire and hotel business. By all accounts, Brown was a miser, living in one of his Brown Hotel rooms, paying his staff as little as possible, and wearing an ancient tuxedo on the few occasions he could be persuaded to make public appearances to accept the gratitude of those on whom he bestowed his largesse. When told that his white shirt showed through the moth holes in his sleeves and he needed to buy a new tuxedo, he quickly remedied the situation with a black ink pen!

He never married, although he had a lady friend of whom he was very fond. His sole aim in life was to make money, and truly, everything he touched turned a profit — except his racing stable. It was the only luxury he allowed himself, although his domineering ways cost him the services of more than one good trainer. Exactly when Brown got into Thoroughbreds no one I ever talked to knew. The story Brown told was that a friend asked him to up the bidding on some horses being run through the sales at Saratoga and soon thereafter Brown "just happened" to find himself the reluctant owner of several likely racing prospects. He bought a farm and raced under the non de course "Brown Hotel Stables." The penny-pinching, curmudgeonish Brown loved his horses with a passion, although he was acutely allergic to them and visits to the stables left him gasping for breath for days afterward.

More than anything else, he wanted to win the Kentucky Derby. To his credit, he never bought million-dollar horses, determining instead to study the sport and breed his own super horse. Some say that was just Brown's style, to do it all his way. Or maybe he was simply too cheap to buy topnotch stock! He gathered together horsemen and bloodstock experts, a "Hot Stove League," as they called themselves, to discuss Thoroughbred pedigree and breeding, seated around a table in the Brown Hotel's famous coffee shop. As long as Brown lived, his hotel at the corner of Fourth and Broadway was the place to be at Derby time. He was so devoted to the Derby that he named a room in the hotel for each winner — except in 1946. The winner that year was ASSAULT!

Brown was an avid racegoer. He could often be seen with his white poodle, Woozem, in his box at Churchill Downs, where he was also a major stockholder. He never bet more than $20. Just because he was a millionaire, he once told a friend, didn't mean he could afford to live like one.

"He would've crawled up happy in his coffin the day he won the Kentucky Derby," an associate remembered. But it never happened. His Snuzzle finished 16th in 1951 and On His Metal was 10th in 1961. Brown did amass a roomful of trophies, the best of which are displayed in the Kentucky Derby Museum's Trophy Room. Through his J. Graham Brown Foundation, he funded the Kentucky Derby Museum. 75,000 people went there annually when the museum was a one-room concrete block structure adjoining Churchill Downs. The two-story, $7.5 million museum that replaced it in 1985 was his gift to Louisville — and the world.

After the Derby crowd has gone to Baltimore or New York, stop at the Brown Hotel and order a Hot Brown; then go to Churchill Downs and work off the calories cheering for your favorites.

A classic Hot Brown recipe reads like this:

Cheese Sauce

2 Tablespoons butter	1/4 cup grated Cheddar cheese
1/4 cup flour	1/4 cup grated Parmesan cheese
2 cups milk	Worcestershire sauce
	Salt

Melt butter in a saucepan; blend in flour. Add milk, cheeses and seasonings to taste, stirring constantly until smooth and thickened. Set aside.

Fixins

8 slices homemade white bread
1/2 pound thinly sliced turkey
8 slices tomato
8 slices bacon or shaved country ham
Parmesan cheese

Toast bread, cut in triangles and arrange in individual baking dishes; it is impossible to transfer a Hot Brown from a baking pan to a plate in one piece. Mound on the turkey. Cover with the hot cheese sauce and top that with a slice of tomato, a strip of partially cooked bacon or country ham. Sprinkle with Parmesan cheese and bake at 400 degrees until lightly brown and bubbly. Garnish with parsley and serve with a warning that the dishes are hot!

WATERMELON RIND PICKLES

Served in little crocks, these tart, translucent tidbits pucker your mouth just right, especially when the entree they accompany is very rich or salty. They appear so often on Bluegrass buffet tables and are so seldom recognized, I feel it my duty to include them here:

Pick the thickest watermelon rind you can find. Trim the green skin and pink fruit from the melon and cut the rind into two-bite chunks. Cover with lime water, made by adding one tablespoon slaked lime to 1 quart water. Let stand overnight. Drain, rinse and cover with cold water; cook until tender but not soft. Drain. Combine 7 cups sugar with 2 cups real cider vinegar, 1/2 teaspoon oil of clove, 1/2 teaspoon oil of cinnamon and 1 lemon, thinly sliced. Heat to boiling. Pour syrup over the rind and let stand overnight. Drain off syrup, heat and pour over rind again. On the third day, heat rind in the syrup until transparent. Pack in sterilized jars. Cover with boiling syrup and seal. These are best served cold.

BURGOO

After two years of going through receptionists quicker than you could blink, the Kentucky Derby Museum was finally blessed with the skills and dedication of Julie Henry. She could courteously answer more phone lines than any person I ever knew. Because the angriest, most demanding caller never flustered her, I nicknamed her "Jewels." Many a day, especially at Derby time, Julie would buzz me and say, "Lynn, I don't understand what this person wants, so I'm sending the call to you." One late-April morning the caller was a thoroughly confused California newspaper reporter. A reader had enquired about the value of a horseshoe, one that came off a Derby winner during the Depression. She couldn't remember the horses' name but it began with a "B" and had something to do with food. The answer had to be the 1932 winner, Burgoo King.

Of course I couldn't appraise the shoe for her. First of all, how could anyone prove, at this late date, that it belonged to the Derby winner? To make my point I told her about grooms on Bluegrass farms who took used shoes and rested them gently on the backs of great horses for half a minute, then sold them to gullible tourists.

"This shoe come off Man o' War," they would truthfully state, and pick up a dollar for their enterprising ways.

She laughed at my story and then asked, "But what is burgoo and why name a horse in its honor?"

We Kentuckians take our food seriously, I told her. It has HERITAGE, just like the horses.

"I see," she said, "but WHAT IS BURGOO?"

Derby was a week away. I had calls waiting and people standing in line at my door. Should I describe it as a soup? A stew? A way of life? I could pull out an old recipe that included squirrel, possum and rabbit, plus a list of ingredients half the length of my arm and read it to her but time was of the essence.

"Burgoo," I said "is road kill and vegetables." And so I was quoted in the newspaper!

I owe part of the complete answer to that question to the late racing writer and consummate gentleman, Charles R. Koch. Charlie grew up near the old Latonia Race Track and remembered childhood trips to the backside where E. R. Bradley's green and white Idle Hour Farm's colors loomed large. Bradley's horses' names all began with the letter "B." The colt in question was named for the "Burgoo King" of Lexington, James T. Looney, a chef whose talents fed the elite at Bradley's Idle Hour Farm charity benefits. Looney also sold burgoo from his concession stand at the old Lexington Trotting Track, where he made it up in batches big enough to feed 5,000 people. He claimed his recipe, and the 500-gallon copper kettle, previously used to make gunpowder, into which he put a ton of ingredients, came from Gus Jaubert.

The *Dictionary of American Regional English* says the word "burgoo," derived from the Arabic for "burghul," cracked wheat, was an old sailors' term for porridge or sea soup. "The fog was as thick as burgoo," gives an idea of the consistency of the stuff they ate. The word migrated inland with the pioneers and meant a feast furnished by hunters and fisherman, with everything — fish, meat and fowl — compounded into a vast stew.

The 1944 *Chicago Daily News* described burgoo as such an ancient Kentucky dish that no two people tell the same story of its origin or give you the same recipe for fixing it. Amen. The most fanciful burgoo story says it was invented by Monsieur Jaubert, a Frenchman who rode with Gen. John Hunt Morgan, and was popular during Reconstruction when food was scarce, because blackbirds were the main ingredient. Those who recite this legend claim it can be spelled "burgout," just to prove how French its origins really are. Others say the name developed because a tongue-tied cavalryman tried to say "bird-stew." *The American Heritage Cookbook* calls it a Kentucky dish, made of hens, squirrels, beef, hogs, lambs, and a wide assortment of vegetables with seasonings; served at picnics, horse sales, church suppers and on Derby Day. That it certainly is. Very highfalutin folks have even suggested that burgoo is the "mess of pottage" for which the Bible says Esau sold his birthright. Without the Biblical recipe we don't know, and frankly, that may be stretching history a bit.

There is in Kentucky an ancient and peculiar organization known as The Honorable Order of Kentucky Colonels. It dates back to the beginnings of the Commonwealth when governor Isaac Shelby bestowed the title of Colonel on his son-in-law and those who enlisted in his regiment in the War of 1812. Later governors commissioned "Colonels" to act as their bodyguards — politics always was "the damndest" in Kentucky! Colonels wore uniforms and were present at official functions. Since that time, every governor has issued commissions to deserving recipients.

The modern philanthropic organization was created in 1931

by a group of Colonels who met in Louisville on Derby Eve. Even in hard times, men came back home on the first Saturday in May. Today they hold a banquet on Derby Eve at the Galt House in Louisville and the Barbecue on Sunday at Wickland, home of three Kentucky governors, in Bardstown. Here, until his death in 1985, the second "Burgoo King" was Columbus R. Barnes. C. R.'s recipe makes 150 servings and begins with three rules: 1) Never get in a rush, simmer at all times and never let burgoo come to a boil, except at first. 2) Keep well stirred at all times. 3) Other than one pound of salt, do not add seasonings until about four hours before serving. "C. R." was the first "Burgoo King" who had to contend with Health Department regulations. He brewed his burgoo continuously for 36 hours because there weren't enough iceboxes in Bardstown to refrigerate the stuff, as required by law, if it sat overnight. Men stirred the pots and tended the wood fires constantly, keeping the stew at that agreeable simmer until it was served.

> Ingredients for 150 servings: 8 pounds of pork, 1 pound of veal, 6 pounds breast of lamb, 30 pounds beef, 20 pounds hens, 20 pounds turtle meat, 1 1/2 gallons tomato puree, 1 pound barley, a gallon diced turnips, 1 gallon whole cut white corn, 10 pounds onions, 20 green peppers, 1 gallon sliced carrots, 5 pounds cabbage, 1 gallon diced okra, 1 gallon diced celery, 1 gallon hull-out cranberry beans, 1 gallon small chopped mushrooms, 3 pounds Irish potatoes.

> To which are added the following seasonings: 1 oz. black pepper, 6 ozs. horseradish roots, 1 oz. Italian seasoning, 1/4 oz. oregano, 1 cup chopped parsley, 1 oz. chili seasoning, 1 pound salt, 1/4 cup Worchestershire sauce, 1/2 oz. bay leaves and 10 pods red pepper, both well pulverized.

Thirty hours before serving time — that's 6 AM Saturday if you expect guests to be hungry at noon on Sunday — place chicken and turtle meat in pot: simmer until meat falls off bone. At 1 PM put in the rest of the meat. When its done, lift the meat out of the stock, cool, chop meat and remove all the bones and fat; return meat to stock and simmer all night. Start preparing the vegetables and add them to the stock about 8 AM Sunday morning. First add to stock 1 1/2 gallons tomato puree, then take out a sufficient amount of stock into a pan to simmer the barley, watching it carefully and stirring to keep it from sticking. When it is tender, set it aside and do no add to main pot until 11 AM Sunday. Add the seasonings, except for the parsley, to the main pot after the barley stock has been removed. KEEP STIRRING, NEVER LET IT COME TO A HARD BOIL. Sample for correct seasoning. At 11 AM add the barley and the parsley. Continue stirring until noon.

•If you're not up to doing it from scratch, or don't know 149 people to share the recipe with, buy it by the quart at Mike Best's, 4894 Brownsboro Center, Louisville, KY 40207. "There are no varmints in our stew," Mike tells customers. They used to make a big batch at Derby, then they started getting requests for it at Christmas. Now they keep it on hand year round, but if you're coming from somewhere else (he can't ship it), call ahead, (502) 896-2516. It's $7.50 a quart and freezes well. Indeed, like love, it is better the second time around. For big orders, give him 7-10 days notice. Around Derby and Christmas, two weeks advance notice is even smarter.

SOUL FOOD

Soul food, not a dish but a deeply satisfying (fat content notwithstanding) ethnic experience, traces its roots to the very beginnings of Southern racetracks. Ironically, racetrack soul food's recorded history begins at Saratoga in upstate New York because of the influence of chef George Crum. Crum was the son of an African-German-Spanish Kentucky-born jockey named Abe Speck and a Stockbridge Indian woman. Crum and his sister-in-law, Aunt Kate (Mrs. Catherine Weeks), were the chef de cuisine and cook at Moon's, a famous Saratoga restaurant that opened in 1853. Crum had learned how to cook from a Frenchman who employed him as a guide in the Adirondacks. It was said of Crum that he could take anything edible and transform it into a dish fit for royalty. If diners dared to return one of Crum's culinary masterpieces to the kitchen he turned it into an indigestible concoction and sent it back, enjoying his victim's indignation no end. From such chefery came the masterpiece which defines American's uniquely nomadic lifestyle.

When a disgruntled diner returned french fried potatoes to the kitchen with instructions to slice them thinner and fry them longer Crum reacted with his typical arrogance. He sliced potatoes paper thin, bundled them in a napkin and dropped them in ice water. Half an hour later he dumped the chilled slices into a kettle of boiling grease. He salted the curly crisps and sent them out to the table, then waited for the disgruntled diner to depart. Instead, the diner ordered more. Other patrons followed suit. The next day, Crum's potato chips, called Saratoga Chips, were on every table.

Crum opened his own restaurant where he charged prices almost as high as those paid in New York City. Long lines of guests, waiting for tables, amused themselves playing the seasonal Saratoga pastime, Fly-Lo, gambling on whose lump of honey-coated sugar a fly would first land!

There were notices barring Negroes from the grounds of Saratoga — out of deference to Southern visitors — a Yankee turf writer explained. Except in the all-white men's clubs, the ban was never enforced because African American jockeys, grooms and trainers were the backbone of Southern racing stables. Southerners brought their own cooks with them to Saratoga as bland Yankee cooking was considered unpalatable and would have ruined their appetites and destroyed their morale in no time flat. The long-held Southern custom of early morning breakfasts at the track became popular at Saratoga in the 1870s, becoming especially important the summer after anti-gambling forces closed the Casino gaming rooms and restaurant in 1908.

An 1892 map of the Louisville Jockey Club, as Churchill Downs was then known, shows 23 on-site kitchens, an old racetrack term referring to the buildings where grooms and exercise riders slept and ate. The cooks who ruled these domains were usually African American. Oldtimers still remember how good the food was back then. Fire marshals eventually called a halt to stable cookery and a way of life passed into memory. Churchill's last backside chef was James "Pork Chop" Doyle, today a Downs' employee whose incomparable barbecuing style is legendary.

•Jay's Cafeteria at 1812 West Muhammad Ali is where owner Frank Foster has done soul food for 21 years. Telephone (502) 583-2534 for carry-out and catering. Frank says his regular customers are too busy Derby week to drop by, so there's room for out-of-towners. But either get there early or prepare stand in the gently moving line.

•Good country cooking is getting so hard to come by, it's almost an endangered species. Leave Louisville and go across the bridge to New Albany, In., and the line around South Side Inn at 114 E. Main Street will tell you you're in the right place. The interior has, as one food critic put it, "seen better days," but the food, prices, can't be beat. They're open 11 AM to 8 PM Monday through Saturday.

•The Brownsboro General Store is a family enterprise that still features gas pumps as part of its decor. You can also buy good work boots there if you've a mind to. Dinner entrees and desserts — everything is made from scratch — are served from a steam table, or you can order a sandwich for lunch, then mosey around the place, which is filled with great Kentucky-made "stuff." Go out of Louisville on I-71 and turn left at the Brownsboro exit or take Highway 42, turn right at Covered Bridge Road and keep on bearing right. If you get lost, call (502) 241-8689 and ask Kent, Susan, Judy or Ed for directions.

GRITS

Grits, which take their name from "gyrt," the Middle English word for bran, are coarsely ground hulled kernels of mature white or yellow dried corn. Grits is/are an acquired taste. It helps if you grew up eating them. Without butter, red-eye gravy, eggs and sausage, they is/are good for you. But they get even better if you doctor them up a bit.

Grits Pudding

1 cup grits	2 eggs
2 cups milk, boiling	1/4 teaspoon pepper
2 cups water, boiling	2 tablespoons butter
1 1/2 teaspoons salt	

Cook grits in salted boiling water and milk until quite thick. Remove from heat and beat in the eggs. Add pepper. Turn into a buttered baking dish, dot with butter and bake at 350 for an hour or until firm. This is a very bland, pale dish that can be scooped onto a breakfast plate and used to sop up the yolk of a sunnyside up egg or counterbalance salty country ham. Or you can make grits simply wonderful by adding 1 1/2 cups grated Cheddar cheese and 2 teaspoons of Worcestershire to the mixture before baking. Heavenly stuff — especially the light brown crust.

•This recipe comes from *The Farmington Cookbook — The Official Hostess and Derby Entertainment Guide*. If you never get any closer to Kentucky horse racing than this 358-page cookbook, now in its sixth printing, you will have lived well.

IN THE HOME STRETCH

Fruits and vegetables, especially strawberries, asparagus and Bibb lettuce, color and harmonize the Derby buffet. Never take vegetables seriously unless the hostess tells you she grew them "on the farm." Then take her seriously. Asparagus and strawberry beds require time and deep roots to produce abundantly. Storebought strawberries, large but tasteless, are nothing like real strawberries, raised in correctly maintained beds. Asparagus, fresh from the garden, is a luxury requiring almost as much commitment as raising a Derby horse.

The Bibb family were among the first settlers of Frankfort. One of their number developed Bibb lettuce — fragile heads of tender leaves, best when joined by avocado or tomato slices in a delicate vinaigrette dressing. Fresh strawberries dipped in powdered sugar cleanse the palate before dessert, which always means chocolate.

DERBY PIE ®

Derby-Pie ® is undoubtedly the thoroughbred of culinary creations. The name is trademarked and registered, just like a Thoroughbred's. If you race your pie, in jest or in public, under that name, you will hear from third generation pie-maker, Alan Rupp's, lawyer tout de suite.

Rupp's grandparents, Walter and Leaudra Kern, were just traveling through Louisville in the 1950s when they took over the management of Melrose Inn, a restaurant that was the last stop on the old two-lane Highway 42, before subdivision-less farm land stretched forever. Today, their Derby Pie® recipe is a corporate secret their grandson zealously guards. The real stuff is served, preferably warm with a dollop of whipping cream, in some of Louisville's best restaurants. It is also available, boxed, ready to eat, at selected grocery stores.

FIRST SATURDAY IN MAY PIE

In the days before lips tattooing and blood-typing, it was possible to substitute one Thoroughbred for another, and win by subterfuge. Running a ringer wiped out more than one bettor and bookmaker a hundred years ago. This recipe for a "ringer" comes from Historic Homes' *Kentucky Heritage Recipes*.

2 eggs - beat slightly
1/2 cup butter - melt and cool
1/2 tsp salt
1 cup sugar
1 cup chopped pecans or walnuts
1 tablespoon Bourbon or 1 teaspoon vanilla

1/2 cup flour
1 cup chocolate pieces

Mix ingredients in order given. Pour into unbaked pie crust.

Bake one half hour at 350. Serve warm with whipped cream.

CHESS PIE

Chess pie is difficult to describe. I once heard an eminent Virginia historian explain that its name is what Northerners thought Southerners were saying when asked the name of their delicious sugar-butter concoction. What he said Southerners were really saying was, "It's jest pie" — they didn't have a name for it! "Jest pie" or chess pie, like bourbon balls, can be controversial stuff. Rose Lyons, owner of Midway, Ky.'s, 19th Century Holly Hill Inn, has written a most tactful introduction to her recipe. "Without starting a war among all our friends, who all feel theirs is the best ever recipe, we would like to claim this recipe as our all time favorite."

1/2 cup melted butter	1 1/2 teaspoons lemon juice
1 1/2 cups sugar	1 teaspoon vanilla extract
1 tablespoon flour	1 unbaked 9" pie shell
3 eggs	

Mix all the ingredients until well blended. Pour into the pastry shell and bake at 350 degrees for 35 minutes.

BOURBON BALLS

Two lifelong friends of my acquaintance, Louisvillian Ramelle "Pat" Patterson and Jean Bell, who was born, raised and still lives in the family home near New Castle, Ky., sat at lunch in the Kentucky Derby Museum Cafe shortly after Derby. Their guest was a young New Yorker, newly arrived at Churchill Downs, wide-eyed as a pilgrim in Mecca. She loved Thoroughbred racing and wanted to know everything there was to know about Kentucky. Pat and Jean explained each dish and potable, making country ham and beaten biscuits sound like manna from heaven. For dessert, Pat suggested a slice of Chocolate Chip Pecan Bourbon pie.

"If you want something just as good and easier to make," Pat volunteered, "I'll give you Mother's recipe for bourbon balls."

As she listed every ingredient, Jean nodded in agreement, the way music lovers nod in time to a well-played symphony. Lillian Maguire Patterson's recipe reads like this:

1 pound confectioner's sugar	1 teaspoon vanilla
5 1/2 Tablespoons butter	1/4 teaspoon salt
2 Tablespoons Kentucky bourbon	1/2 ounce paraffin
1 3/4 cups pecans	

2 8-ounce packages Baker's Semi-Sweet Chocolate

So far so good — indeed, absolutely delicious. Pat proceeded. "Cover the pecans with bourbon in a glass jar and let them marinate overnight or several days prior to use."

Jean reacted with wide-eyed amazement. "Why Pat," she exclaimed loudly, "you never told me you soaked your nuts!"

Pat raised her voice and declared, as only an Irish daughter of the Bluegrass can de-clare, "Mother always soaked her nuts!"

Conversations at nearby tables stopped. Heads turned. Natives knew Bluegrass wars have started over less significant culinary details. Decorum required a truce while dining with Northerners so instruction could proceed:

Cream butter in a bowl. Add sugar and bourbon alternately until well mixed and concoction is easy to handle. Add vanilla and salt and mix well. Press enough mixture around drained pecans to cover and shape into a ball. Place ball on a waxed paper-lined flat tray. Chill overnight. Melt paraffin in double boiler. Add chocolate, stir until melted and well-blended with paraffin. A teaspoon of butter may be added at this point. Dip chilled bourbon balls in the chocolate and place on waxed paper. Let chocolate firm and dry. Store in a container in a cool area or refrigerate.

Jean Bell's recipe deserves telling here because it is so simple.

1 pound box powdered sugar - sifted
2 tablespoons coffee cream
1 tablespoon + 1 teaspoon Kentucky Bourbon (Jean recommends Makers Mark if it is available in your area)
8 1-oz. squares melted unsweetened chocolate
Pecan halves

Combine the first three ingredients. Knead until mixture is well blended and does not stick to hands, adding Bourbon and/or sugar until mixture reaches desired consistency. Shape into balls around pecan half. Put on wax paper and chill. Melt chocolate in double boiler. Using a fork, dip each ball of candy into chocolate, gently tapping fork on the side of the pan to remove excess chocolate. Slide bourbon ball from fork onto wax paper.

There is a personal quality that makes Kentucky food unique. The history of *Rebecca-Ruth Candy* is almost as good as the bourbon balls they still shape by hand in Frankfort, Ky., and ship just about everywhere.

At the end of World War I, just as racing was getting back on its feet, two Kentucky belles, Ruth Hanly and Rebecca Gooch, turned Christmas candy making into a full-time business and were soon swamped with orders. When Prohibition closed the Old Frankfort Hotel barroom, the manager rented it to them. Ruth paid $10 for a large imported marble slab, made especially for the barroom of the Capitol Hotel that had burned in 1917. Visitors followed their noses for a peek at the genteel candy makers and a taste of the best mint candy anywhere.

The ladies bought a car, mounted sandwich-board advertising on the side, and sold candy all around central Kentucky. Eventually Ruth married, sold her interest in the company to Rebecca and moved to Ft. Thomas, Ky., where she went right on making candy, because folks in Cincinnati loved her confections as much as Kentuckians did. First, family misfortune brought Ruth back to Frankfort, then her husband, Douglas Booe, died. With an infant son and two nieces to care for, Ruth didn't get back into candy making until 1929, the year Rebecca Gooch married and offered to sell her former partner the thriving business. Mrs. Booe transferred production to her house in Jett, Ky., and hired a teenager named Edna Robbins to man the marble slab. When the Depression curtailed both orders and production, Ruth Booe developed new candies. Then her home burned to the ground; only the marble slab survived the blaze. Local banks turned down her requests for a loan to rebuild, so with $50 she borrowed from a hotel housekeeper, she put herself back into the candy business a fourth time.

For Derby visitors, Ruth dressed like a Southern belle and stationed herself in the lobby of the Kentucky Hotel, passing out samples of *Rebecca-Ruth* candies, sold by the piece or the box. Sighting gov. Ruby Laffoon in the crowd, she offered him the only available chair, right next to her booth. People eager to shake the governor's hand found Ruth Booe's mint Kentucky Colonels equally irresistible.

Just before World War II, she developed the secret recipe for her 100 proof bourbon balls, after a friend remarked that *Rebecca-Ruth* mints and a sip of bourbon were the two best-tasting things in the world. She called them "Bourbon Kentucky Colonels." When sugar was rationed, Ruth Booe's friends brought in their personal supplies for her to convert to candy. After a review by *New York Times* food editor, Jane Nickerson, brought the candy company national recognition in 1947, *Rebecca-Ruth* became an American institution. Thirty thousand pounds of sugar becomes *Rebecca-Ruth* candy every year. As for the marble slab and Edna Robbins, they're both still going strong. The factory store, where visitors can see the candy being made January through October, is located at 112 E. Second Street in downtown Frankfort, Ky. In November and December, tours stop. The staff must concentrate on playing Santa Claus for its world wide clientele. The *Rebecca-Ruth* catalogue warns customers: "Please understand. . . the chocolates we ship are very fresh and should be eaten immediately upon opening." What better reason could there be for not hiding a box of *Rebecca-Ruths* from oneself?

Candy can be ordered by calling 1-800-444-3766, but the most appealing way to appreciate *Rebecca-Ruth* is to take the Versailles Road off I-64 near Frankfort, on the way to Keeneland, and look for a small white building on the right, one mile south of the turnoff. The sign out front says "Bourbon Candy." The aroma inside says "heaven." It is possibly the best introduction to the Bluegrass one could wish for.

MODJESKAS

If spirited sweets are not your cup of tea, stick to Modjeskas, named for the Polish actress who was Kentucky Derby founder, Colonel Meriwether Lewis Clark's celebrity Derby guest. Louisville confectioner Anton Busath created this candy to celebrate Helena Modjeska's 1883 appearance in Ibsen's "A Doll's House" at the Macauley Theatre. Modjeska was a favorite of Louisville audiences, and presumably, Derby-goers as well.

For more than 50 years, Busath's held the trademark on the pillow-shaped sweet, but when his 4th Street shop burned in 1947, Busath left the candy business forever. As with most things foreign, the name eventually took on a new pronunciation and spelling. Nowadays they are often called "majestics," implying a sense of royalty they certainly deserve!

Finding a recipe for the divine dainty is not easy. Most cookbooks endorse a Modjeska look-alike made by dipping marshmallow halves in caramel. In no way does it compare to the real thing which requires perfect timing and nimble wrists, according to *The Courier-Journal*'s Assistant Food Editor Alice Colombo, whose true-to-life version is infinitely more rewarding to consume.

Assemble the ingredients for the marshmallow:
vegetable oil for pan
1 T. confectioners' sugar, sifted
1 T. corn starch
1 cup granulated sugar
1 1/2 teaspoon corn starch
3/4 cup water
2 T. unflavored gelatin
1/2 teaspoon vanilla
1 egg white
More confectioners' sugar for dusting the marshmallow

Caramel Ingredients:

2 cups sugar	2 cups heavy cream
1 1/4 cups white corn syrup	2 T. butter
1 teaspoon vanilla	

Begin with the marshmallow: Lightly oil a 9"x13"x2" baking pan. Combine confectioners' sugar and cornstarch. Dust pan with mixture. Over medium heat, combine the granulated sugar and the corn syrup with about half the water. Stir constantly until the sugar is dissolved. Bring to a boil without stirring, then increase the heat until syrup reaches 260 degrees on a candy thermometer (hard-ball stage).

In a small pan, soften the gelatin in the remaining water for 5 to 10 minutes. Set the pan over simmering water and, whisking constantly, dissolve the gelatin. Add vanilla. Stir.

Beat egg whites until stiff.

Whisk dissolved gelatin into syrup. Whisking continuously, gradually pour syrup over stiffly-beaten egg white. Continue whisking until marshmallow mixture is a white opaque mass that is thick enough to hold its shape.

Pour into prepared pan and smooth flat. Let set for several hours or over night.

With the tip of a knife coax the marshmallow away from the edge of the pan. Dust the candy board with confectioners' sugar and turn marshmallow onto it. Cut into one inch squares and let dry for about an hour.

To make caramel:

In a smooth nonporous metal 3 to 4 quart saucepan, combine

white corn syrup, sugar, and 1 cup cream. Place over low heat, stirring gently, until sugar has dissolved.

Place remaining cup of cream in a small pan and hear separately, Increase heat to medium . Bring sugar and syrup mixture to a rolling boil Slowly drizzle the hot cream into boiling mixture, stirring and keeping the mixture constantly at a boil. Insert warmed thermometer in the pan. Adjust heat so syrup bubbles steadily and gently. Stop stirring. When the thermometer reaches 238 to 240 degrees (this will take 30 to 40 minutes) remove from heat and stir in butter and vanilla.

What follows is not child's play. The caramel must be kept warn enough for dipping but not so hot it melts the marshmallow. Allow caramel to stand for 10-15 minutes before starting to dip the marshmallows. Butter or oil clean surface, such as a cookie sheet. Drop each marshmallow into caramel, working it gently with a fork until it is completely covered. Lift it out with a fork, pulling it over the edge of the pan so excess caramel runs back into the pan.; The caramel can be placed in a pan of hot water to keep it from hardening, but speed is of the essence.

Put each piece of a buttered surface. When set, wrap each piece separately in a square of waxed paper. Makes about 4 dozens.

Modjeskas look like plump bed pillow. They melt in your mouth and stay on your hips forever. If you believe candy making is an art best left to professionals, Muth's Candies sell Modjeskas for $10.50 a pound and ship them anywhere. Their 75-year-old store is located at 630 East Market Street in Louisville. Telephone (502) 585-2952 or 1-800-55MUTHS.

MINT JULEPS

Always save the best for last. And pray you do it justice. By such strong cords of tradition is the mint julep bound to racing in Kentucky, there might be some who would argue that without bourbon or mint, the first Saturday in May couldn't happen. There are as many recipes for making a mint julep as there are old families in the Bluegrass. Boast in print that you have the only correct recipe for a mint julep and wait for testy letters to appear in your mailbox!

A quintessential Kentuckian, Vice-President Alben Barkley, best described the drink: "A mint julep is not the product of a formula. It is a ceremony and must be performed by a gentleman possessing a true sense of the artistic, a deep reverence for the ingredients, and a proper appreciation of the occasion. It is a rite that must not be entrusted to a novice, statistician or Yankee. It is a heritage of the Old South, an emblem of hospitality, and a vehicle in which noble minds can travel together upon the flower-strewn paths of happy and congenial thought."

It is not a solitary drink, but one that must be carefully timed and planned for, made in quantity and shared with friends. Juleps are warm weather drinks, not at all suitable for cold weather because the glass won't frost properly. The ingredients sound so simple, yet think how difficult they were to obtain on a summer day 150 year ago. That's what makes the drink an aristocrat — one of those cultural wonders which only happens in the South.

Pick mint when it is young. Use only the tenderest leaves. Have good Kentucky bourbon whiskey on hand. The real stuff is made from a fermented mash of corn, rye and barley malt that must be at least 51 percent corn. All bourbons are aged in new charred white-oak barrels to give them a unique, smokey taste. How long they are aged makes all the difference. Bourbon cannot be hurried, by law or custom.

A basic recipe reads like this:

Make a simple syrup by boiling 2 cups sugar and 2 cups water, without stirring, for five minutes. Fill a jar loosely with fresh mint sprigs and refrigerate for a day. Discard the mint. You now have mint syrup.

Frost 16 glasses by wetting them and placing them in a freezer overnight. An hour before serving time, especially if the humidity is tablespoon of mint syrup and two ounces of bourbon. Garnish with a fresh sprig of mint and serve immediately.

According to purists, the only way a mint julep can be savored is from a sterling silver julep cup, preferably won by one's horses at Keeneland and so engraved. The first record of these beaker- shaped vessels being given as racing prizes comes from Chester, England in 1609. The patient work and luck of racing Thoroughbreds usually requires a lifetime to put together a sizable collection. Lacking that bit of status, sterling julep cups can be purchased from two Kentucky sources, Wakefield-Scearce in Shelbyville and Brown-Waterhouse-Kaiser, Inc. in Louisville. Both firms have been making cups for Keeneland and Churchill Downs for generations.

•Eighteen years ago, Louisvillian Becky Biesel thought Derby entertaining should be casual and fun. Today her Party Kits & Equestrian Gifts is an international mail order service for a wide range of

party goods, from Derby Logo paper plates to silk scarves and silks colors custom-painted on crystal. She does gift baskets all year long and can ship Derby Pie® around the world. Order a Party Kits & Equestrian Gifts catalogue by calling (502) 425-2126 or 1-800-99-DERBYor writing P. O. Box 7831, Louisville 40257-0831.
Visit the store right off Shelbyville Road in Lyndon, Ky., at 8007 Vinecrest Avenue. You don't have to fight mall traffic to get there.

•Julep cups in all sizes, shapes and styles are a specialty of Louisvillian Betty Gist's distinctive Executive Shopping Service. Call her at (502) 897-EXEC, to order one exquisitely gift-wrapped cup for a special guest or as many as you need done up for a corporate occasion. Betty can be relied upon to provide you and your organization with tasteful visibility.

•Brown-Waterhouse-Kaiser's showroom is located in the classic Heyburn Building at Fourth and Broadway, directly across from the Brown Hotel. The telephone number is (502) 583-2728.

•The Wakefield-Scearce Antique Gallery, the source of julep cups given as trophies at Keeneland, is worth a trip to Kentucky just to see. The grand and spacious building, once a 19th Century girls' school named Science Hill Academy, is located at 525 Washington Street in Shelbyville, 30 miles east of Louisville. The telephone number is (502) 633-4382. If you're looking for something special, the person to call there is Shirley Hays.

•Science Hill Academy founder, Julia H. Tevis, was one of the most brilliant educators Kentucky ever nurtured. In her autobiography she wrote "I went into a kitchen once. I didn't like it!" Judging from Julia's portrait, someone who knew what she was doing ran her kitchen, because Julia certainly ate well. Science Hill Inn, next to Wakefield-Scearce, serves the most wonderful Kentucky food in a room reminiscent of the great dining halls of colonial Virginia. The Sunday buffet, for which reservations are a must, merits a drive from anywhere. As with most good things, it's a family operation and Donna, Ellen or Terry Gill are usually on hand to greet you. The telephone number is (502) 633-2825. A real family recipe book, *What I like Best About Dining With The Gills*, is available there for $7.95.

•If learning how to cook racing fare is high on your list, a one-stop resource center for lessons, equipment, affordable china, individual Hot Brown dishes and crockery is Butler's Barrow at 3738 Lexington Road in Louisville. The number is (502) 893-5003 or 1-800-249-3595. Their color catalog is a feast for the eyes. Butler's

Barrow is an off-shoot of Dolfinger's, located right next door. This old Louisville institution prides itself on having served local families since 1863. The silver and china at Dolfinger's is fit for the Queen, should she ever come racing in Kentucky again.

•Heading east, up Shelbyville Road and a left turn away, at 127 N. Sherrin Avenue is Carol and Gary Campbell's Gourmet Cottage, a rambling 19th Century store. These seasoned cooks specialize in cooking equipment. If what you're cooking is larger than the pots they stock, it should probably be barbecued in a pit outside. Their telephone number is (502) 893-6700.

•Cookbooks can be ordered from the following sources:

Farmington Cookbook
Farmington
3033 Bardstown Road
Louisville, KY 40205, telephone (502) 452-9920
$12.70 by mail, $10.95 + sales tax at their gift shop

Fifth Edition Historic Homes Kentucky Heritage Recipes
Locust Grove Historic Home
561 Blankenbaker Lane
Louisville, KY 40207, telephone (502) 897-9845
$4.00 + tax and mailing charge

Bluegrass Winners can be ordered from The Garden Club of Lexington
P.O. Box 22091
Lexington, KY 40522
$17.95 + $3.00 postage and handling. Ky. residents add $1.08 for sales tax

Kentucky Derby Museum Cookbook
Kentucky Derby Museum
704 Central Avenue
Louisville, KY 40208
Call 1-800-593-3729
$22.OO plus $5.50 for out-of-state shipment
Instate shipping is $28.82, including the 6% tax.
The museum accepts Mastercard, VISA, American Express and Discover

CORDONBLUEGRASS

Published by the Junior League of Louisville, $16.95 + sales tax and UPS shipping charges, can be ordered from Hawley-Cooke Booksellers by calling (502) 893-0133 or 1-800-844-READ. If you're in Louisville, this delicious, well-staffed bookstore has cafes at its Shelbyville Road Plaza and Gardiner Lane Shopping Center, and very accommodating hours for browsers and book lovers.

The Holly Hill Inn Cookbook, a must-have, at $11.95, is available at Holly Hill Inn in Midway by calling (606) 846-4732 and at Bluegrass-area bookstores.

Kentucky Thoroughbreds

I love the Hoss from Hoof to Head,
From Head to Hoof and Tail to Mane.
I love the Hoss, as I have said
From Head to Hoof and back again.

I love my God the first of all,
Then Him that perished on the Cross
and next my Wife and then I fall
Down on my knees and Love the Hoss.

James Whitcomb Riley

Chapter Fourteen

Racetrack Relics

If you bought the August 31, 1955 program at Washington Park and trashed it after the Swaps-Nashua match race, left your Kentucky Derby souvenir mint julep glass for track maintenance to dispose of and cashed all your Secretariat win tickets, collecting racetrack effluent is probably not your cup of tea. For most Thoroughbred fans the excitement of horse racing is in the next finish. But, for a growing legion of devotees and investors, the totes, programs, badges and glasses — and the memories they evoke — are what counts. So they haunt flea markets, trade shows and yard sales, hoping to find bits and pieces of racing's past, buying, swapping and trading racing's treasures.

"It's a Walter Mitty thing," says California stockbroker Gary Medeiros, who wrote racetracks asking for programs when he was hospitalized with polio as a child. Today a computer printout of his collection stretches the length of two football fields.

"Genuine racing heroes" is how Medeiros classifies the horses of the early years, as he looks for rare programs from the likes of Phar Lap and Colin. Tracks have always attracted "stoopers" who go through the castaways looking for uncashed pari-mutuels. The most short-lived paper in the world — before the advent of the fast-food wrapper — was the tote ticket. In pre-computer times, each track's betting tickets were specially printed on coded paper to prevent counterfeiting. As with postage stamps, every ticket reveals its history only to those who understand the codes.

For Louisville newspaperman Myron Estes, the lure at Churchill Downs was racing and Kentucky Derby mint julep glasses — not the antique silver beakers cherished by Bluegrass gentry, but the aluminum, Bakelite and utility glass examples with acid-etched or painted-on ice frosting that Libbey first produced for Churchill Downs in 1939. Derby creator M. Lewis Clark made the slow-sippin' southern drink a tradition by serving it to his Jockey Club guests, but some smart fellow whose name is lost to history realized it was keeping too many bettors away from the action on the track so he put the drink in a cheap, decorated glass and hawked it in the grandstands.

That first year, 6000 glasses were ordered for the 50-cent drink that was 75 cents if you bought the glass. Today one of those 1939 glasses can set you back more than $1300 — not a bad return for a quarter investment! For the next two years — to cut down on breakage — the souvenir julep glass was aluminum. With the onset of World War II, metals and glassmaking chemicals were diverted to munitions manufacture and Bakelite was given the contract to provide glasses made of Beetleware. These colorful 5-inch plastic tumblers were sold during the "streetcar Derby" years, so-called because of wartime transportation restrictions, and nobody knows what the total production was. Beetleware julep glasses have been found in nine springtime hues, all — except a rare banana-yellow one — speckled like eggs. The only identifying mark is the horseshoe logo on both sides near the rim. Bidding on Beetleware julep glasses starts at $1000. Today no collector has a complete set. The yellow example once belonged to Estes, before his collection was stolen four years prior to his death in 1994.

The 1945 Derby was postponed until after V-E Day. A June race date may explain why, for the first time, the glass was artificially "frosted" before it ever left the factory, so even if the ice in the glass melted, the julep had a cool, appealing look.

Art was always a part of Kentucky's Bluegrass heritage. It was no accident that Swiss painter Edward Troye chose Lexington as his base of operations and is buried in the Georgetown, Ky., cemetery within walking distance of what were once some of the great early horse farms. Troye's paintings — the few pieces that are not already in private collections and museums — are eagerly sought after by those able to pay the five-figure price tags.

Collecting original Thoroughbred horse art can be very expensive — especially when you choose to buy the Thoroughbred first. But even multi-millionaires have to stand in line to have their prized possessions painted by the likes of Lexington artist Julie Wear, who works only from life and will not paint a champion once his winter coat starts growing in.

Most artists today, Julie Wear included, do what Troye did and reproduce their masterpieces in limited edition prints. Whether you choose programs, glasses or art, collecting's a great way to get started in the horse business.

Chapter Fifteen

Could You Please Tell Me?

Q - According to family history, my great-grandfather trained horses and won the Derby. Nobody remembers the name of the horse. Is the information available at the track?

A - A hundred years ago, several fashionable, big-money races were called Derbys. The term wasn't just reserved for Thoroughbred racing either. Standardbreds had their Derbys too. If your roots are in the midwest or New England, chances are that great-grandpa was a trotting horse man. If he had Kentucky roots he may indeed have trained a Derby entrant, but without the name of the horse — or the dates he was active as a trainer — it's like looking for a needle in a haystack. Even the Downs' official Derby Press Book only lists the names of trainers from 1908 on. Before 1900 the owner often trained his own horses, so only the owner's and the rider's name were listed in racing records.

If you want to look for great-grandpa, find out as much specific information as you can, then go to Keeneland and ask for the racing newspapers that cover the years he could have been active in the sport. The print is fine and the paper is thin, but these papers covered American racing from A to Z.

Q - My relative rode in the Derby. How can I find out more about him? My ancestor was a jockey. I don't think he ever rode in the Derby but I want to find information on him. Where can I look?

A - A jockey's professional life was often brief, so don't expect to find much, but chances are good that you will find something. Churchill Downs Press Book lists every jockey who had a Derby mount, all the way back to 1875. Old publications such as *Goodwin's* or *Crick's* (available at the Keeneland Library) also list jockeys by name. In the back of the *Daily Racing Form Book*, an annual publication, there is a listing of jockeys active that year. The Keeneland Library has complete sets of these volumes.

Q - My ancestor once owned a racetrack. I'm pretty sure it was Churchill Downs. Does the track have any information about him?

A - This question came up, usually in a long, handwritten letter, with more stories than you can shake a stick at. Usually ancestors owned the track and lost it, true to sporting form, in a card game or a roll of the dice. I suspect many of these stories have a grain of truth in them and that great-great grandpa did indeed own a stake in a small track somewhere.

If you have similar legends hanging from the branches of your family tree, examine old town records and newspapers close to where great-great grandpa lived. See if you turn up any information about a racetrack in the vicinity. Land ownership can be verified at county courthouses. Remember that racing has always depended on domestic peace, a good economy and an adequate supply of horses.

Q - Tell me about the mule that won the Derby?

A - I don't know why people think a mule ever won the Derby, but I was asked the question a number of times. I will concede that 1907 Derby winner, Pink Star, does look mulish in his winner's circle photo but it was a rainy day, the camera angle was all wrong, etc., etc., etc.

Q - I bought a horse I think is a Thoroughbred but I didn't get papers. He has a lip tattoo. How do I find out his name? I want to register a Thoroughbred I just bought? How do I go about getting the information I need?

A - The Jockey Club Information Systems telephone number is 1-800-333-1778. This user-friendly, Kentucky-based arm of The Jockey Club is a gold mine of information about Thoroughbred pedigree. Information about registering a Thoroughbred is available from The Jockey Club. The telephone number is 1-800-444-8521.

Q - How do I register silks?

A - There is a myth that the registry of racing colors is a permanent, semi-sacred act ennobled by time and The Jockey Club. One may register one's racing colors with that organization if one chooses. One must register with that organization if one races in New York. In Kentucky, silks are described on a license approved by the Kentucky State Racing Commission, 4063 Iron Works Pike, Lexington, KY 40511, (606) 254-7021. *A History of Racing Silks* — if you want to design your own — by Gayle C. Herbert, is available at most Bluegrass bookstores.

DERBY DATA

Q - My grandfather had box seats for Derby. After he died, my grandmother inherited them, but at her death, my mother didn't get them. Why not?

A - For decades, once the Derby became a fixture, the same Louis-

A - For decades, once the Derby became a fixture, the same Louisville families had the same boxes at the Derby. "My Derby Box" was one of those standard references people spoke about to establish their rank in the order of the racing and social universe. The better the box, the older and more distinguished one's ancestry, or so it seemed. Families did not own those boxes, they did pay for them year after year, usually using them only on Oaks and Derby Day. The rest of the time they sat idle, which wasn't good for business. By the mid-1980s, the Downs was losing money on everything but the Derby. Unprofitable traditions had to go. And go they did, much to the horror of families who thought of "their" Derby box an inalienable right. Shock waves went through the community as families were notified of the change, then they consoled themselves by saying the race was not really enjoyable anymore — what with so many outsiders horning in — and began giving wonderful Derby parties at home.

Q - Does that mean there's a chance I might be able to gets seats for the Derby? How?

A - Option A is to go through channels at the track. Write a letter stating the number of tickets you want. Ask for the best available seats, but don't be specific. They will seat you where they can. You will get a form letter acknowledging your request. Sometime between November and March, the form letter will state, you will hear from them. A ticket will cost between $50 and $100, depending on location. This will get you a grandstand or clubhouse seat, which may or may not be under cover. While it doesn't pay to be specific about the location you want, you can embellish your letter with any facts that make you stand out from the crowd — maybe you're a Thoroughbred owner or celebrating your 100th birthday. Nothing guarantees you preferential treatment, but every little bit helps. The Downs is handicap-accessible at ground level, but on Derby day that area is wall-to-wall people. Because the grandstand is so old, getting around requires some physical agility. Even in expensive seats, a trip to a rest room can be a long trek. Note your limitations in your letter and be honest. The staff do try to accommodate as many people as possible. Address your inquiry to: Ms. Harriet Howard, Churchill Downs Derby Ticket Office, 700 Central Avenue, Louisville, KY 40208.

Be advised: For $30 you can buy a general admission ticket to the Derby the day of the race. The ticket gets you into the standing room only area by the track and the clubhouse paddock area. You cannot bring chairs into this area. $20 buys an infield ticket, where chairs, coolers and non-alcoholic drinks can be brought in. GLASS CONTAINERS ARE NOT PERMITTED. Guards stationed at the gates have the right to search containers and toss prohibited alcohol in a big dumpster, so prepare accordingly. BECAUSE OF FIRE REGULATIONS FANS WITH LAWN CHAIRS MUST ENTER AT GATE 3 and REMAIN IN THE INFIELD.

Option B is to go underground. In states where it is legal to sell a ticket for more than its face value, ticket brokers offer a wide range of tickets for sporting events. Beginning early in the year, they advertise their 1-800 numbers in the Classified sections of local newspapers. Expect to pay roughly three times the face value of the ticket for this service. Oddly enough, the earlier in the season you purchase tickets, the more you're likely to pay for them. That's the price of buying peace of mind and the ability to make travel arrangements well ahead of time. The closer you come to Derby, the more sellers are willing to bargain. They would rather take less and get something, than be left with worthless stubs of paper as the rose garland is settled around the winner's neck. Be warned: scalping — selling tickets at more than face value — is illegal in Kentucky. So you take a chance when you do it.

Option C, tailor-made for groups, is to let experienced local professional tour planners do your footwork for you. It is essential that you give these businesses at least nine months advance notice if your group or organization plans to visit at Derby time. Remember too that Keeneland races in April and October. Churchill's Spring Meet opens the last Saturday in April and the meet lasts until the Fourth of July. The Fall Meet begins late in October and runs through Thanksgiving, so enjoying the sport is by no means limited to the first Saturday in May.

•Tours Plus owner Susan Langford is the great-great-great-great-niece of Daniel Boone. Small group tours are her forte. If she and her capable staff can't get you around Kentucky, nobody can. Call her at 502-897-3789.

•VISITOURS is a family-owned company that has specialized in making visitors feel welcome for almost 20 years. Especially at Derby time, when preplanning is essential, their expertise can make all the difference in the world. Grace K. Duckworth is the person to talk to there. Her number is (502) 456-2774.

Q - How handicap accessible is Churchill Downs?

A - The track complies with Federal standards, providing close-in parking and access to seating and rest rooms throughout the facility.

Q - I hear that public parking near the Downs on Derby Day nightmarish. How do I get there?

A - Unless you get to the track before dawn, parking is ever bit as impossible, and expensive, as you've been told. Plan to park at the Fairgrounds and use public transportation. TARC (Transit Authority of River City) has thought out all the details for you. Call 502-585-1234 for more information and schedules.

Q - What do I wear to the Derby?

A - Whatever keeps you warm, dry and comfortable. If you want to go for fashion too, that can be challenging, but not impossible, especially if you have covered seating. Remember, Stephen Foster was a Yankee on a brief visit to Bardstown when he wrote "the sun shines bright on my Old Kentucky Home. . ." He didn't stick around long enough to experience spring weather, and if he had, it would not have been fit for song lyrics. We **hope** the sun will shine bright on the appointed day, but, in 1989, it snowed shortly before the race, as it did during Derby week 1993. Derby '94 was a gully washer, after a lovely week of warm spring weather. 1995 was the picture of perfection. Take a tip from the jockeys and wear silks. When it gets really hot, the lightweight silk jacket that kept you warm at breakfast can be slung over your shoulders.

•Some of the best silk separates come from Talbots, which produces a full line of classic clothing early every spring for their resort catalog. Sizes range from a petit 2 through a standard 20. If you don't know Talbots, (there are stores in Louisville and Lexington) call 1-800-882-5268. They answer the phone 24 hours a day.

•For special occasion and formal wear — especially stunning "belle of the ball" gowns — SHE is a Louisville tradition. The store is located in St. Matthews at 211 Clover Lane and the number is (502) 897-5361.

A hat is not required for admission, but Derby seems to be the one day of the year when women enjoy wearing hats, and some very extravagant productions show up every year. If the Derby has an official milliner, it's Frank Olive. He loves putting his customers in just the right hat, and appreciates hearing from ladies who own his creations. Obviously, the larger the hat, the more it will be noticed, either because you look great or you're blocking someone's view. The downside of "le grand chapeau" is keeping it on your head. The track is windy and you will need — trust me — your hands free for more essential activities.

No matter how expensive your seats, you still have to walk and climb stairs to get to them. High heels and tight skirts can be inconvenient, uncomfortable and exhausting. In spite of the fact that Churchill recently replaced ancient bricks with smooth pavers along some walkways, stiletto heels get caught in cracks. Wear 'em and weep.

Men can dress pretty much as they please. A jacket and a tie are the safest bet for all but the least expensive seats. Be warned, if you are invited to lunch in the Stakes Room, a perk that comes with running a horse in a stakes races, a sports coat and NO BLUEJEANS is the minimum dress requirement. I once watched a very genteel and gracious multi-millionaire — his horse had done well in the Derby that year — hunched over his table looking like a thrift shop refugee. No one had told him about the dress code and a jacket four sizes too large had been hastily secured for him. Too embarrassed to stand up, he stayed in his chair the entire afternoon and sent his wife to the buffet for his lunch.

Q - What about dress codes on other days at the Downs?
A - Anything goes at ground level — the infield, paddock area and Silks Restaurant — but all food service areas above the first floor that require reservations have, and enforce, dress codes. NO shorts, running suits, sweat pants, spandex, T-shirts, tank tops, midriff or halter tops are permitted in the Skye Terrace where men must wear collared shirts and dress slacks. Women must wear dresses, skirts or dress slacks. The Eclipse Dining Room or Eclipse Terrace requires men to wear jackets. Women wear dresses, skirts or dress slacks. Neither jeans or shorts are permitted. The ultra-posh and very private Turf Club does not allow women to wear pants. Men must be suitably suited or tied and blazered.

Q - Any words about the Press Box?
A - The fifth floor Press Box is not accessible to the general public. It is the media's domain, off limits to those without press passes. While a tie is not required, men must wear long pants — no Bermuda shorts allowed.

Q - I would never go to the Derby, but a day at Keeneland sounds like fun. How do I dress?
A - One of the saddest, and coldest, men I ever met was a New York

trainer who flew into Lexington the last week in April to run a stakes horse at Keeneland. It was a balmy 72 degrees when he got on the plane, so he dressed for the sunny South. By the second race, the snow was coming down so hard we could barely see the track. It didn't last, but the wind did. The trainer had to be coaxed out of his seat to saddle his stakes prospect. Lexington tends to be cool and wet in April. Again, conservative silks are a good rule at this race-course where men must wear jackets, ties and collared shirts (no turtlenecks) in the very private Keeneland Club and ladies do not wear pants in any of the dining rooms. Only a fashionable few wear hats or designer clothes. You see a lot of khaki, tweed, pearls and good leather around the paddock.

A note to men: Keeneland employees responsible for visitor services wear a distinctive "Keeneland green" dress jacket, so if you resemble them you may be asked for directions or assistance you are not prepared to give.

Q - I'd love to be part of Derby but it sounds like too long a day for me. Is there an alternative?

A - Churchill Downs advertises a sunrise buffet every morning there's racing during Derby week. The track is usually closed ("dark" in racing lingo) on Monday of Derby week. Late in 1994, ARAMARK swallowed up Harry M. Stevens Company — the people who made hot dogs and baseball synonymous in the 1800s. They don't take reservations for the Spring Meet until the first Monday in April, so mark your calendar accordingly. Their number is 502-636-3351.

The doors of the Eclipse Dining Room open at 7 AM. Park in the lot on Central Avenue and follow the signs through the main gate. The dining room is handicap accessible but it's wise to mention you're using a wheel chair so seating can be arranged accordingly.

The Eclipse Room opens onto the terrace. Churchill's Director of Publicity, Tony Terry, is master of ceremonies for the event. If you can only attend one day, Tony recommends Tuesday and Wednesday, the days Derby contenders put in their last major workout. Turf workouts follow the dirt workouts after the dirt course closes at 10 AM.

Q - This sounds like a great program. Does it only happen during Derby week?

A - After Derby, the buffet becomes a regular Saturday morning event for the rest of the Spring Meet. Book your reservations and dress casually in comfortable shoes and a jogging suit or jeans, because there's an added bonus after Derby. Two tours, at 8 AM and 9 AM, are available on a first-come, first-served basis. To be sure of getting a spot on the shuttle bus that takes you to the backside, sign up for the tour when you get to the Eclipse Room. This is a 20 minute walking tour. Flash bulbs and umbrellas are prohibited. Use a video camera to record your memories here.

Q - Is there anything else I should know about racetrack rules and etiquette? What about cameras?

A - It is always wise to inquire about using a flash camera around horses. If you are told by racetrack guides, guards or trainers not to take pictures of horses, either on the backside or in the paddock, for everyone's safety, heed their request.

THOROUGHBREDS ARE NOT PETS. THEY DO BITE. MORE THAN ONE PERSON HAS BEEN DRIVEN TO THE EMERGENCY ROOM BECAUSE THEY TRIED TO FEED OR PET A THOROUGHBRED.

Q - I'm coming to Louisville for Derby, staying with friends, and want to experience one of those truly fabulous Derby breakfasts I hear so much about. How can I do that?

A - The oldest, and one of the best, Derby Day breakfasts is hosted by Historic Homes Foundation, alternating between their two historic sites, Locust Grove and Farmington. The feasting begins at 9 AM, and ends at noon, in tents set up in the garden area of these imposing houses. Reservations are taken year around for this event. Write Anne Bertrand, Historic Homes Foundation, Whitehall, 3110 Lexington Road, Louisville, KY 40206 or call 502-899-5079. The cost is $75 per person, $90 for a reserved seat, or a private tent, with food and libations, is available for groups of 25 or more at $100 per person. Anne says she'll guarantee beautiful weather — most of the time.

Q - Can I visit the Kentucky Derby Museum between races on Oaks and Derby Day?

A - It is closed both Oaks and Derby Day to accommodate private parties for members and patrons. Information about the museum, which is located adjacent to the Downs parking lot at 704 Central Avenue, can be obtained by calling 502-637-1111.

Q - What is the Kentucky Derby Festival?

A - Think back, circa 1873, when the Churchills asked local hotelmen and streetcar company owners to invest in a racetrack. Think again, circa 1902, when Matt Winn was trying to round up $40,000 from local business interests to keep the Derby on track. Now, imagine them succeeding beyond their wildest dreams. That's the Kentucky Derby Festival today. Thousands of local volunteers and businesses support Festival activities, which turn the Derby into a month-long civic celebration and raise thousands of dollars for charity. Information about Festival activities can be obtained by calling (502) 584-6383. The Derby Festival's Internet Home Page address is: http://www.iglou.com/KyDerbyFestival.

Chapter Sixteen

Resource and Gift Guide

Thoroughbred Magazines, Libraries and Pedigree Data

•No book about American Thoroughbred racing can be written without reference to a newspaper Benjamin Gratz Bruce brought out in Lexington the year the first Kentucky Derby was run. First called *The Kentucky Livestock Record*, the weekly publication covered agriculture, sports and political news as well as the arts. In 1895, the name was changed to *The Thoroughbred Record*, which continued until 1986, when it became an upscale monthly. In 1988 *The Thoroughbred Record* merged with *The Thoroughbred Times*, a weekly newspaper still based in Lexington. For subscription information contact:

> *Thoroughbred Times*
> P.O. Box 8237
> Lexington, KY 50433
> (606) 260-9800

•*The Blood-Horse* is the weekly publication of the Thoroughbred Owners and Breeders Association, Inc. For subscription information contact:

> *The Blood-Horse*
> P.O. Box 4038
> Lexington, KY 40544-4038
> (606) 278-2361 or 1-800-866-2361

•*Backstretch Magazine*, a bi-monthly publication, is the official magazine of the United Thoroughbred Trainers of America. For subscription information contact:

> Editorial Office
> 142 Breckinridge Lane
> Louisville, KY 40207
> (502) 893-0025 or 1-800-325-3487

•For a just plain beautiful magazine that covers all aspects of Thoroughbred life, the publication to subscribe to is *SPUR -The maga-*

zine of Equestrian and Country Life. This long-lived publication is a who's who and what's what guide to the best horse sports have to offer — from carriage driving, to art, to Pony Club. For subscription information call 1-800-458-4010.

•Thoroughbred Racing Communications, Inc. — a national media relations office funded by The Jockey Club, Breeders' Cup Ltd. and The Thoroughbred Racing Association — publishes the *TRC Media Update*, a newsletter filled with news, features, racing statistics and historical data about personalities in the sport. Since 1994 TRC has published *Post to Post — A World of Thoroughbreds for Kids*. For subscription information contact:

TRC
40 East 52nd Street
New York, NY 10022
(212) 371-5910

•*The Kentucky Thoroughbred Farm Directory* is published annually by the Kentucky Thoroughbred Farm Manager's Club, 600 Elsmere Park , Lexington, KY 40508-1604. The Directory has over 200 pages of photographs, maps and information about Bluegrass horse farms, along with industry-related advertisements. To order the Directory call (606) 253-1764.

•The Keeneland Library — still maintained as a gentleman's library but very amenable to researchers — is open from 8:30 to 4:30 weekdays, except during race meets when it closes to the public at 11:00 AM. It is located at Keeneland Race Course on Versailles Road across from the Bluegrass Airport. The mailing address is U.S. Highway 60, P.O. Box 1690, Lexington, KY 40592-1690, telephone (606) 254-3412.

•Those traveling through Virginia horse country should visit The National Sporting Library at 301 Washington Street in Middleburg, Virginia, 22117. Librarian Laura Rose can answer questions about several centuries of equine books and sport horse records. The telephone number is (703) 687-6542. Hours are 10 to 4 weekdays, or by appointment.

•For tracing Thoroughbred pedigrees of over 900 outstanding American horses from the foundation sires through 1972 the AMERICAN THOROUGHBRED SIRE LINES wall chart is an excellent aid. The 3 1/2 x 5 foot colored chart is available from:

Equine Enterprises
P O Box 807
Smithtown, NY 11787

•The Jockey Club Information Systems Inc. is a source for information about Thoroughbred registration, pedigree and racing records. This user-friendly resource is located at 821 Corporate Drive, Lexington, KY, 40503, (606) 224-2800 or 1-800-333-1778.

Horse/Iron Horse Museums

•The Kentucky Derby Museum offers a wide variety of educational experiences for adults and children, has an on-site restaurant, and can be rented for daytime and evening events. Guided tours of Churchill Downs are available, following the multi-image show, every hour on the half-hour, beginning at 9:30 AM. The museum is open 9 to 5 every day except Thanksgiving, Christmas, and the first Friday and Saturday in May. For more information, contact:

Kentucky Derby Museum
704 Central Avenue
Louisville, KY 40208
(502) 637-1111

•The Kentucky Horse Park is a horse lover's dream come true — the one place a tourist can really get close to horses because more than 40 breeds call the Horse Park home. Located at Exit 120, off Interstate 75, the facility offers horse events, the International Museum of the Horse, the Horse Center and the Winner's Circle Gift Shop. They have an education department which offer seminars and workshops on everything from art to equine management, geared to people who want "hands on" experience with horses. For information about hours, events, trail rides and special programs contact:

The Kentucky Horse Park
4089 Iron Works Pike
Lexington, KY 40511
1-800-568-8813

•The Kentucky Railway Museum, Inc. is located at New Haven, Ky., below Bardstown. Information about hours and schedules, during the months the museum is open, can be obtained by calling (502) 549-5470 or 1-800-272-0152.

•Located 15 miles from Lexington, the Bluegrass Scenic Railroad offers tourists a 90-minute journey through the Bluegrass, along the old Louisville Southern Railroad line. Halfway through the trip you can disembark and walk to "Young's High Bridge," a railroad trestle built in 1888, 280 feet above the Kentucky River. For information about the museum's hours and special trips, call 1-800-755-2476 or 1-606-873-2476.

Professional Associations

•Information about jockey licensing can be obtained from the Kentucky State Racing Commission, 4063 Iron Works Pike, Lexington, KY 40511, (606) 254-7021 or the Jockeys' Guild, Lexington Financial Center, 250 W. Main Street, Lexington, KY 40507, (606) 259-3211. Information about subscriptions to *The Jockey News*, the Guild's newsletter, can be obtained by writing: *The Jockey News*, 7183 Cascade Drive, Boise, ID 83704-8633.

•For information about careers in farriery contact The American Farrier's Association, 4059 Iron Works Pike, Lexington, KY 40511, (606) 233-7411.

•The American Association of Equine Practitioners is headquartered at the Kentucky Horse Park, 4075 Iron Works Pike, Lexington, KY 40511, (606) 233-0147. If you're traveling or moving, and you're new to an area, call 1-800-GETADVM and they'll give you a list of vets available in your area.

•The UNITED THOROUGHBRED TRAINERS OF AMERICA, INC., based in Louisville, Ky., is a service organization that exists for the benefit of Thoroughbred trainers, owners, and other racing industry personnel. Call (502) 893-0025 or 1-800-325-3487 for more information about the benefits offered by the UTTA, INC.

Collecting Racetracks Relics and Mementos

•An excellent reference guide for Kentucky Derby glass collectors is William Friedberg's *Pictorial Price Guide and Handbook for Official Collectibles of the Kentucky Derby, Preakness, Belmont and Breeders' Cup.* The book is available at the Kentucky Derby Museum and area bookstores or it can be ordered from Bill at 462 Hillcreek Road, Shepherdsville, KY 40165, (502) 957-4039.

•Horse Star Cards are creator John Ball's answer to baseball cards, except that his heroes are horses and jockeys. The cards are sold at racetracks and thoroughbred gift shops or they can be ordered through HSC, P.O. Box 444, Buckner, KY 40010, telephone (502) 222-1200.

•Collectors Gallery, filled with all kinds of horse art, is conveniently located at 1501 Versailles Road, between Lexington and Keeneland. The number is (606) 233-1121 or 1-800-626-6927. The gallery is family-owned by gentlemen who know their horses.

•Right next door, at 1505 Versailles Road, Nags 'n Rags has an incredible variety of horse wares, housewares and human wears. The telephone number is (606) 233-1927. They also have a shop at the Bluegrass Airport across from Keeneland.

•About the time Churchill Downs was getting started, Lexington built its first "shopping mall" on West Main Street. Today that block-long, block-wide site in the heart of Lexington is known as Victorian Square, a remarkable multistory renovation that houses a diversity of shops and restaurants, just as it did when it was built. Two stores here, A Touch of Kentucky, telephone (606) 255-0954 and The Gift Horse Emporium, telephone (606) 252-4993, are delightful sources for Kentucky foods, jewelry, books, and baby gifts. Children are never too young to learn about horses.